TRICKSTERS
AND
PUNKS OF ASIA

WORLD CLASS SHORTCUTS

SPUNK
IMPRINT

FAST TRACK

PUBLISHING

TRICKSTERS & PUNKS OF ASIA
World Class Shortcuts

© Phil Nicks 2010

First Edition, 2010 (Special limited punk edition)

Published by Fast Track Publishing, Thailand
Email: fasttrackpublishing@gmail.com
Website: www.fasttrackpublishing.com
Fax (Hong Kong): +852-3010-9769

ISBN: 978-616-90336-2-2

BIC Subject Categories:

1F (Asia); AVGU (Punk, New Wave & Indie); AVH
(Musicians); HPQ (Ethics & Moral Philosophy); JFCA
(Popular Culture); JFHF (Folklore, Myths & Legends);
JMP (Abnormal Psychology); JMS (The Self, Ego,
Identity & Personality)

Designed and printed in Thailand

"Come to me*
Come unto me*
All ye that labour
You that are heavily laden
Coz everything hurts"

The Fall

* - Humanists and outsider artists only!

CONTENTS

Chapter 7: Tricksters in Love & Lust

APPENDIX

ACKNOWLEDGMENTS

Thanks to the following individuals for their contributions and support:

Crispin Sartwell, (www.crispinsartwell.com) for his permission to reproduce his essay about the history of punk in Chapter 1, Part II

Damiana L. Eugenio, *"Mother of Philippine Folklore"*, for trickster tales from the Philippines

Paul Bradley and Finbarr Murphy, for an abundant supply of tunes and ideas

Tom Schwab, for his knowledge of psychology

Mr Robert, for his views about *Tricksters of The Night*

Gary, for the photograph on the back cover from Jo and Dickie's *White Wedding*

Mike, for assistance with Chapters 2 and 3

Kristina Lindell, renowned scholar of Asian folklore

Logoboom, for the photograph on the front cover

Dr. Ngo Van Doanh, Editor in Chief of Southeast Asian Studies

Harry Palmer, founder of Avatar, for knowledge about cults

Paiboon Publishing, for continuous support and enlightened publishing practice

PREFACE

Welcome to the world of punks and tricksters! I trust you will enjoy the experience as I lead you along this wonderful, and occasionally frightening, journey through the underworld.

I have benefited enormously from this research, so I feel compelled to share it with you, whether you are a nonconformist outsider or an insider seeking a glimpse of a different world.

This book is in two parts: firstly, a detailed introduction about essence of punk, tricksters, outsiders and corruption from a global perspective. Please note that punk is a global phenomenon and trickster tales are etched in tribal folklore on every continent. The second part of the book is a collection of tales and articles about tricksters and punks from Asia. Some of the stories originate from folklore, while others are contemporary.

The trickster tales are compartmentalized into three zones: business, spirituality and love. I am experienced in all three areas, but most of all, love. Among the trickster tales is my personal account of investigating the faith – and fake – healers of the Philippines. I also wrote about the pitfalls of getting a book published, and tales of reckless living.

This book is the result of an amazing evolutionary journey which I am sharing with you. The starting point, punk - like a meandering river – led me to tricksters, then outsiders, before culminating at the estuary, genius. Genius, which is congruent with true love, is covered in *Genius of Love* (refer to page 248).

During my study of punk, I researched three notorious non-conformists: punk rocker, Joe Strummer from the
Clash; anarchist writer George Orwell; and radio deejay
John Peel. All three individuals were raised in loveless
middle class families. Each of these men had integrity,
passion and humanist intent. And one of these men – John
Peel – attended my christening ceremony in 1960.

Most people misunderstand the ethos of punk, which
is understandable, so I have attempted to redress this im-
balance. Punk is about individuality, freedom, passion and
intent to express ourselves truthfully. Punks are outsiders
who also embrace the trickster archetype.

I love authentic punk music, especially the music of
Talking Heads, David Byrne and B52s which is uplifting
and apolitical. My other favorites are The Fall, The Clash
and the Dead Kennedys. The latter two bands are classified
as far-left punk. For a list of recommended songs, refer to
my discography on pages 232 - 233. Plug any song title
into Youtube.com's search engine, then click and enjoy!

Why, you may ask, did I choose to research the subject
of punk in the first place? Here's what happened....

In May 2008 I met an Australian ex-monk called Eric
at a local café in Chiang Mai. He claimed that when he
stayed in Thailand - during his mid twenties - he heard
a voice in his head saying *"A man must be the embodi-
ment of his own ideals."* Eric said he thought immediately
of cherry yogurt. *"So I knew I had to go to Pondicherry
to study yoga in India."* He said. So he began his spiritual quest, and for the following thirty years he lived as a
monk.

Two days later I met Eric outside my guesthouse. *"You look like a punk monk!"* he said. I ignored Eric as I dismounted my motorbike and walked upstairs to my room, contemplating his remark.

I had shaved my head, so perhaps that's where Eric's notion of a monk came from? Also I was wearing red shorts and a sweaty vest after taking rigorous exercise. But Eric was probably unaware of the significance of punk philosophy in my life.

I began to like the concept – or archetype – of *The Punk Monk*. So the next day I phoned Eric and thanked him for giving me the *"Punk Monk"* idea. "You should write a book entitled, *The Wisdom of the Punk Monk*." he replied. I sensed that Eric was mocking me; but I loved the idea. Indeed Eric was my catalyst for writing the story entitled *The Birth of the Punk Monk* (pages 160 - 176).

In June 2008 I met a local Australian evolutionary astrologer who interpreted my astrological chart. The astrologer emphasized the influence of the planetoid Chiron – known as *The Wounded Healer* - upon my life. You will learn more about Chiron later.

I researched the astrological significance of Chiron and was surprised to discover its uncanny congruence with the *"Punk Monk"* idea. … Astrologer Jessica Adams links Chiron with *"sheer brazen nerve"* of punk attitude… And so the seeded concept of the archetypal Punk Monk – nonconformist outsider and multidimensional genius - began its process of germination…

On pages 124 – 131 you are able to evaluate yourself using the *Punk Monk Quotient*. This index is a measure of enlightened non-conformity. By the way, this system is not accredited by any established professional organization, although I can rubber-stamp it!

I must forewarn you that Chapter 3 (about outsiders) is a bit heavy. The world needs outsiders, radical artists and geniuses. There are plenty of money-grabbing insiders out there, doing their bit to destroy the planet; but not enough people who are willing to risk ridicule and create something unique, something to make the world a better place to live in.

Perhaps there are three people in the history of mankind noted for resisting corruption altogether: Jesus, Buddha and Luciani, *"the Smiling Pope"* (John Paul I).

Jesus was supposedly crucified. And there is firm evidence available that Pope John Paul I was poisoned for his attempt to clean up the corruption inside the Vatican. Trust a person who smiles; but beware those who look mean! The death of Luciani clearly touched the punk movement, since Patti Smith wrote *Wave*, and The Fall wrote *Hey Luciani* – both songs in honour of the Smiling Pope. Asians, and particularly Thais, smile a lot because they are genuinely open-hearted and kind people.

Phil Nicks
Email: info@philnicks.com
January 2010

PS: If you like this book, *Genius of Love* (page 248) is probably for you, too.

PART I:
INTRODUCTION

CHAPTER 1

PUNK: ESSENCE, MYTH AND REALITY

The meaning of *"punk"* is universally misunderstood, like the punks themselves. Dictionary definitions of the word are unanimously negative and confused. Therefore the purpose of this chapter is to clarify the essence of punk to reveal the punk aspect of *The Punk Monk* archetype.

The perceived ethos of punk has been bastardized by myriad factions jumping on the band wagon. These groups include nihilistic troublemakers; commercial predators vying the quick buck; extremists from both ends of the political spectrum; middle class pantomime performers and art school kids; intellectual voyeurs; and socially excluded freaks with nowhere else to call home.

Misrepresentation of this non-conformist subculture by mainstream authorities is inevitable because its essence has been buried underneath a mountain of excrement. Somewhere under this stinking mound lies a philosophy worthy of recognition.

The following case is typical. A request for specific books was emailed to a book dealer. One of the books on the *"wish list"* was *The Philosophy of Punk* by Craig O'Hara. The book trader replied with the following post-script:

> *"The only title unknown to me is The Philosophy of Punk. I guess that even punks have ideas; but I am not sure if they add up to philosophy; but then, what the hell do I know?"*

Perhaps the book trader had been indoctrinated by omnipresent toxic definitions of *"punk"*, such as:

1. Slang a. A young person, especially a member of a rebellious counterculture group b. an inexperienced person
2. Music a. Punk rock b. a punk rocker
3. a Slang: a young man who is the sexual partner of an older man b. Archaic: A prostitute[1]

Many dictionaries define a punk as a worthless person, criminal or prostitute. The official adjective for *"punk"* is defined as low quality or cheap.

The word *"punk"* originated in the sixteenth century when playwright William Shakespeare referred to harlots and strumpets in his play, King Lear.[2] One source states that the word *"punk"* is a derivative of *"Puncture.*[3]*"*

Punk has roots in American Indian shamanism. Punk wood is a slow-burning substance which smolders and creates billows of smoke. The American Indian tribes of the Algonquian family in Delaware used punk wood or crushed cedar bark to make incense or smudge sticks.[27]

Shamans use smudge sticks for spiritual hygiene and energetic protection during ceremonial ritual. The most common ingredient for smudging is sage, which produces plumes of thick white smoke. Smudging clears negative energy and lifts the spirits.

Wood punk incense contains sawdust from the Asian hardwood, machilus. Machilus sawdust is used to make incense because of its propensity to absorb scented essential oils.

16

Wood punk incense is known for stimulating child-hood memories[28] ; and an important aspect of punk is being *"young at heart"* and creatively expressing our "inner child". Many middle class f**k-ups give their money to psychotherapists or hypno-therapists for their guidance while revisiting and expressing their long-lost inner child. Being playful and fun-loving (or seemingly childish) is one of the prerequisite qualities of geniuses.

The cannibalistic Mohawk tribe of Northeast America used to refer to the Algonquian-speaking tribe as *"Adiron-dack"* (which means *"bark-eaters"*) because they ate the bark of white pine trees when food was scarce.[29] Many punk rockers emulate the Mohawks by wearing classic Mohican hairstyles.

There are other connections between punk and tribal-ism which are covered in detail in the following chapter. Punk is associated with the pogo dance which is similar to the *"jumping dance"* adopted by Kenya's Masai tribe. The fierce repetitive rhythms of punk rock often incite strong feelings, opening gateways to cathartic self-expres-sion. Some of the music is primal; and, like primal therapy, it's about re-experiencing and healing the birth trauma by screaming like hell.

Punk was the name given to a type of corn which was eaten by American Indians in Virginia in the seventeenth century.[31] The corn, which was cooked in a broth, had an unpleasant taste. Punk literally means *"ashes"* in Dela-ware Indian language.

Other definitions for the noun, *"punk"* follow: Mis-creant or subversive[4]; a worthless person[5]; nonsense, foolishness[6]; an aggressive and violent young criminal[7]; substance that smolders when ignited, used to light fires[11]; a disrespectful, rude or otherwise unpleasant person[12]; a sissy[13]; a young man who fights and breaks the law[14]; a young man used as a homosexual partner, especially in prison[24]; a style or movement characterized by the adoption of aggressively unconventional and often bizarre or shocking clothing, hairstyles, makeup etc, and the defiance of social norms of behavior, usually associated with punk rock musicians and fans.[25]

Punk is used as an adjective in slang to mean: of poor quality; worthless; weak in spirit or health[5]; bum, cheap.[22]

There is even a verb for the word which supposedly has equally caustic meaning: To insult or intimidate[18].

Synonyms for the word *"punk"* include bad, inadequate, not good[8]; crummy, chintzy, cheesy, bum, sleazy, tinny, cheap[9]; hoodlum, mug, roughneck, rowdy, ruffian, hood.[20]

Punk rock is described as an anti-establishment rock music genre[16]; music played in a fast, loud and aggressive way[17]; type of music with attitude; the kind of music which says *"I don't give a f**k what you think!"*[19]; rock music with deliberately offensive lyrics, expressing anger and social alienation[23]; rock music containing frank and confrontational lyrics.[33]

The names of the punk rock bands surely reveal the essence of the music: *The Undertones, The Damned, Chaos UK, Crass, The Misunderstood* (managed briefly by deejay John Peel), *The Exploited, The Fall, The Pretenders, The Blockheads, Sham 69, The Dead Kennedys, Joy Division, Underworld, and of course, The Clash and The Sex Pistols* (representing 'the yin and yang' of punk rock).

The informal word *"spunk"*, however, has an official meaning which is closer to that of *"punk"*: courage, spirit, nerve[10]. The Sex Pistols – the masters of spunk - released an official bootleg album called *"Spunk"* in 1977.[30] *"Spunk"* is also slang for semen, which has a connection with sexual potency of the American Indian Winnebago Trickster.

Original punks stood for anarchism, idealism, freedom and doing whatever they wanted[15], regardless of societal conventions and taboos.

Punk is the quest for freedom outside mainstream systems. Punk is non-conformist. ***"What the system feeds us today is what the punk movement hates most: Standards".***[21]

Globalization enhances homogeneity by asserting *"World Class"* standards, formulae and regulation. The result is less choice, stifled creativity and massive redistribution of power to the members of the World Trade Organization.

When David Byrne was asked what he feared most about the future, he replied:

"I'm afraid that everything will get homogenized and be the same. I'm also afraid that reason will triumph and that the world will become a place where anyone who doesn't fit that will become unnecessary"
- David Byrne[32]

David Byrne's quote scores a bull's-eye for the real meaning of punk. Punk is really about the individual's creative freedom which overrides limiting rules and regulations, formulaic standards or social conventions.

There are many aspects to punk which include: Making something happen against all odds (such as Sir Bob Geldof's Band Aid); creating something from nothing (or with limited resources); being multi-talented and continuously learning new skills (such as being musician and record producer); being *"Jack of all Trades"*, and maybe master of none; expressing socially-taboo ideas; practicing a trade without formal training, accreditation or licensing; establishing unorthodox systems outside of the conventional system; expressing oneself truthfully and creatively without paying lip service to social conventions; impulsive, spontaneous or bizarre behavior in the *"now"* moment; not having anything to lose; poking fun at authority and busting illusions; being a misunderstood outsider or *"black sheep"*; valuing real originality and unique forms of artistic expression; saying what needs to be said; deploring bigotry, political correctness and other forms of malign judgment, social manipulation and control; honoring and fulfilling our instincts; being unrefined, unorthodox and unconditioned; eccentric, genius and magical; flamboyant joker who stands out from the crowd; facing severe challenges and obstacles; chaotic or damaged; being self-empowered rather than doing things to please others;

individual and unique; being master of our own destiny; taking shortcuts if necessary; and taking responsibility for oneself.

Punk is popularly perceived as an anti-establishment subculture, attracting the entire spectrum of non-conformists from societal outsiders, criminals, the mentally ill, political extremists, anarchists and the long-term unemployed to middle class art students, tertiary-educated philosophers, champagne socialists, *"creatives"*, voyeuristic anthropologists and excitable hacks digging through the dirt. For many people, punk was a fleeting pantomime, but for *"non-conformists with a cause"* it still remains an ideological lifestyle.

The authentic punk mindset is exacerbated by inadequate patriarchal leadership, hypocritical jerks as *"role models"*, poor education, ignorant abusive parents, control freaks and lack of emotional support.

Punk ideology is a vehicle for individuation from the restrictions of autocratic subordination to free expression and empowerment. The individuation process is a term introduced by Carl Gustav Jung to describe the quest for purpose in life, enhanced self awareness and self-actualization (as defined by Maslow).

Individuation is the process of psychological maturity. Individuation is becoming aware of our shadow, our anima and animus (female and male qualities), our personality archetypes and our *"core essence"* or Self.[54] This process results in a unique and self-aware individual with an integrated personality.

The overriding principles of punk are sovereignty of the individual over him or herself, and mastery of the individual's destiny. Personal liberation is achieved by passionate creative self-expression.

The limitation of institutional or corporate structures lies in their formulaic nature and fundamental disregard of an individual's essence. Punk rationale facilitates personal transformation by peeling away layers of conditioned beliefs (or *"bullshit"*) which envelopes an individual's authentic being. If punk has a single rule, it is: *"Be yourself!"*

Punk philosophy leans towards fierce independence; and thus freedom from the constraining forces of mainstream corporate entities which have potential to corrupt artistic expression. This principle is known as Do-It-Yourself (or DIY). DIY-mentality leads to self-empowerment; whereas compliant specialization tends towards tunnel vision and dependence.

The Significance of 1977

The year 1977 represents the time when punk exploded in UK. The Clash wrote a song entitled *1977* and Talking Heads released an album using the same name. On 18 June 1977 The Sex Pistols' defiant *God Save the Queen* became a Number 1 hit single in UK. The year 1977 is profoundly significant for individuals, non-conformists and… both astrologers and wounded healers.

In 1977 a new planet was discovered by astronomer Charles T. Kowal at the Hale Laboratories in California. The planet became known as Chiron, *The Wounded Heal-*

er, due to its energetic resonance with the mythological centaur and the consciousness of Christ. Chiron is described on pages 214 - 216.

The planetoid Chiron was discovered at the zenith of punk rock's influence in UK. Chiron, like punk, has the qualities of a shooting star: urgent, intense and potentially short-lived (like Ian Curtis of Joy Division and Sid Vicious of The Sex Pistols). Also between 1976 and 1978 several underground human rights protests rose to the surface of public consciousness, including gay rights under the leadership of Harvey Milk in America, and the formation of Adult Children of Alcoholics (ACoA).

ACoA is one of many addiction recovery groups which adopt the Twelve Steps principles. The first organization to use the Twelve Steps was Alcoholics Anonymous. These groups are for *"wounded healers"* who suffered during their childhood, typically at the behest of parents who projected their psychological issues onto their children.

Chiron was also discovered during the impetus of the Human Potential Movement: a secular rather than spiritual movement involving self-awareness, self-responsibility (instead of victim consciousness) and conscious living. Chiron is both change agent and wounded healer, linked to the maximization and expression of human potential.[60]

The spirit of punk was present before the 1970s. The American soprano, Florence Foster Jenkins (1868-1944), was famous for her lack of tone, rhythm or singing ability. Jenkins wore elaborate costumes that she designed herself, sometimes appearing in wings and tinsel, and for Clavelitos, throwing flowers into the audience while fluttering a fan and sporting more flowers in her hair. After a crash in a taxicab in 1943 Jenkins found she could sing the F tone as never before; so she rewarded the taxi driver with a box of cigars instead of suing him.[71]

Non-Conformity

Punks are non-conformists, taboo-breakers; and commonly dismissed as social deviants or untouchable outcastes.

Non-conformism has its own scale of authenticity. At the top of the index are psychologically *"centered"* individuals who are earnestly driven to express themselves creatively. These artistically-inclined punks are self-empowered to articulate their heart and soul regardless of external judgment. As the saying goes, *"If you don't like it, f**k off!"*

The punk rock band, The Fall, is the epitome of punk. Its founder Mark E Smith cannot sing, neither can he dance. The uninitiated may dismiss Smith's art as unprofessional, but it works. One of The Fall's collections, entitled *50,000 people cannot be wrong*, alludes to its narrow yet loyal marketplace. Whether his followers are right or wrong, they always come back for more.

The Guardian referred to Mark E Smith as *"a professional outsider and all-round enemy of compromise."* He breaks all known musical conventions, adding a suffix *"uh"* at the end of every lyrical line. Since 1976, in line with his working class ethic, he has printed over 78 albums.[72]

The genius Mark E. Smith (The Fall) is known for his sheer bloody-minded determination to keep his band moving artistically. During The Fall's year of malcontent (1998), Smith's spoken word album entitled *The Post-Nearly Man*, was slammed by New Musical Express magazine, *"You can count the substantial ideas here on the fingers of a Kit-Kat"*.[47] Many Fall fans believed the band was dead. Smith was accused of experiencing midlife crisis after he physically assaulted his remaining band members on stage in New York. Within months of the spoken word album, The Fall surprised everyone with the release of the acclaimed *Marshall Suite*. In true Wile E. Coyote style the music industry witnessed, yet again, the rise of the Phoenix-like Fall.

Outright rebellion, Stalinism and abrasive provocation lie towards the bottom of the non-conformists' authenticity index. These punks are *"rebels without a cause"*[48] and nihilists with intent to smash the entire system.[49] The problem is that most iconoclasts have no feasible alternative system to offer post-meltdown. Anyway, it's smarter to run in tandem old and new systems concurrently until the innovative ideas are grounded into reality.

> *"So much of what's doled out as punk merely amounts to saying I suck, you suck, the world sucks, and who gives a damn – which is, er, ah, somehow insufficient"*
> - Lester Bangs[66]

There are several talented and practical punk bands on both sides of the Atlantic, notably UK's Crass and America's Fugazi. Steve Ignorant and fellow band members of the far-Left band Crass established their own record company, Crass Records. Both bands *"walk their talk"* earnestly and the result is massive success. Ignorant says the intelligence agencies tapped the band's phone lines, indicating that certain elements of the punk movement really posed a threat to the powers that be.[59]

Self-Reinvention

Punks are tricksters with a penchant for self-reinvention. Yes Men dismiss such behavior as 'dodgy', but real punks perceive it as responsibility to realize their personal potential.

The standard 3-step roadmap to instant self-reinvention is:

1. Change your name and physical image
2. Teach yourself a new discipline or skill. Don't worry; formal training, certification or accreditation is not necessary
3. Promote your new art

Within two weeks it's possible to establish a completely new identity and means of living. Attitude and passion for the art is more important than talent.

The endless list of successful name changes includes Johnny Rotten, Joe Strummer, Jello Biafra, Steve Ignorant, Poly Styrene, Sid Vicious, Lene Lovich and Richard Hell. Numerologists attach deep meaning to names and many esoteric practitioners link names with specific energies. For example, the name, Smith, encodes the energy of creativity; perhaps why Robert Smith (The Cure), Mark E. Smith (The Fall) and The Smiths (with Johnny Morrissey) have been so successful with their art.

Punks are multi-colored, multi-talented chameleons with the ability and inclination to metamorphose sporadically. Having nothing to lose facilitates the process of change, as does a passionate urge to express oneself freely.

For example, Raymond Burns who co-founded The Damned in 1976 later overhauled his image as Captain Sensible. The new quirky persona of a joker wearing a red beret underneath spiky peroxide blond hair was bound to entertain. In September 2006 the Captain formed a British political party called "Blah! Party" using the slogan, *"Politics is dead!"* Some 98% of the British electorate judged the Captain's party as politically incorrect. Maybe the captain is ahead of the times or otherwise suited to other kinds of party?

The song *"What's my name?"* by The Clash indicates either identity crisis – am I Joe Strummer, "Woody" or John David Mellor? – Or an urgent desire to individuate and find his real self. Joe Strummer changed his lifestyle (and name) at least twice dropping his previous friends like a lead balloon. Strummer fantasized about being a criminal, and in *"What's my name?"* he assumes the identity of a petty thief.[43]

Authentic punks crave real freedom - the ability to express oneself creatively in a suitable space. The moment we deny our passions in favor of rigid specialization we become vulnerable to enslavement. So ideally there are always other gateways available to access alternative forms of art.

Passion is omnipotent. Qualifications are essentially employment passports. Many punks don't have a stable monthly paycheck, preferring the free-lance work and life on the edge.

Resourcefulness

Creating something out of nothing – without regard for social conventions, rules and taboos - is the ethos of punk.

Many industries are closed to innovative ideas and assert rigid entry barriers. So the punk attitude is, *"OK, let's do it ourselves!"* The output may be quirky and the quality may be rough, but at least the product is out there.

The Orwellian slogan, *"Ending is better than mending,"* is a cultural byline for punk. Safety pins are used to keep ripped clothing intact; used items are recycled or adapted; products are exchanged and skills are bartered. Getting by on a shoestring is the punk way.

The UK punk music scene was ignited by promoter Malcolm Maclaren from the trendy *"Sex"* clothing boutique which he operated with designer Vivienne Westwood. Sex Pistol Johnny Rotten (John Lydon) dressed himself in Westwood's outrageously provocative clothes. Maclaren later managed The Sex Pistols.

In Finsbury Park, London an attractive Afro-Caribbean lady protected herself from a rainstorm. The exotic lady wrapped a carrier bag on her head before confidently braving the severe weather. It was a bizarre spectacle, but she was no slave to restrictive social conventions, and she had the final laugh because her hair remained dry. Now that's punk!

Saying *"You cannot do that!"* to a punk is like a Spanish bullfighter taunting a bull with a red flag. Frank Zappa responded to such comments with true punk attitude; he produced a series of six albums entitled *"You can't do that on stage anymore, Volumes 1 - 6"*. So Zappa ignored his critics' discouraging guidance and instead poked fun at them by using their dispiriting comments for album titles together with evidence that he can still do it on stage!

"Real DIY underground punk rock is still being made. There are still people playing in punk bands, setting up under-funded tours, throwing shows wherever and whenever they can (in San Diego they have 400+ person punk shows in the sewer!). There are also still punks organizing protests and benefit shows, making 'zines, hosting radio shows, starting record labels, living in sh*tty houses or squats (or with their parents)... the mainstream perception of punk may have changed, but I think the heart is still there. Bands like the Marked Men, Resist, Witch Hunt, Gruk, or Death Crisis are still playing and touring, zines like Razorcake and Cometbus are still being printed, groups like the Pyrate Punks are still setting up shows, festivals like Chaos in Tejas and Fest are still taking place, anarchist bookstores and infoshops are still popping up all over the world..."[35]

Originality

Creative expression and originality is the ethos of punk – be yourself and be as outrageous as you wish.

Mark E Smith (The Fall) is the epitome of originality. The Fall has a unique vocal style tagging the *"uh"* suffix onto each lyric. The Fall have been accused of plagiarizing the *"uh"* postfix from Johnny Rotten (Sex Pistols).

"Many people, including John Peel, regard The Fall as the most authentic punk band"
- Tony Fletcher, Jamming magazine[53]

The Fall's counteractive lyrics - conjuring feelings of hopelessness, futility and post-industrial decay - are enmeshed liberally in a caustic monotone rant. And the anarchic musical accompaniment is anti-harmonious and perfectly discordant.

Hedonism

Brazen hedonism is part of the punk lifestyle. Hedonism leads people in different directions, especially sex (serial monogamy or polygamy), drugs (including alcohol) and punk rock 'n' roll.

"The Palace of Excess leads to the Palace of Access"
- The Fall[52]

Perhaps the path to access is the Palace of Excess – an illicit den en route to The Palace of Wisdom.

The mystic poet, William Blake, wrote *"The road of excess leads to The Palace of Wisdom"*. Without experiencing excesses like a fool, we cannot really delineate between balance and excess. So, acts of foolishness are steps towards wisdom.

Experience is the ultimate teacher. The fearful limpet, hiding under his shell, clinging to its host, and who never takes any risks, is ostensibly sensible. Such marine gastropod mollusks are forerunners of the Living Dead.

Appearance

Punk rock has no physical barriers to entry unlike other music genres which pull the sexiest and most fashionable divas, and coolest pedigree studs. As Joe Strummer, says[34], *"If you're ugly, you're in!"*

Ian Drury (of The Blockheads) had a physical disability which necessitated his use of a walking stick. Drury contracted polio at the age of seven during Britain's polio epidemic in 1949.

Ian Drury mocked his physical affliction in the lyrics of the song, Spasticus (Autisticus):

I'm spasticus; I'm autisticus.
I'm spasticus; I'm autisticus.
I'm knobbled on the cobbles;
Cos I hobble when I wobble;
So place your hard-earned peanuts in my tin;
And thank the creator you're not in the state I'm in.
- Ian Drury and The Blockheads

Contrary to popular perception, not all punks are tattooed Mohawks wearing ripped jeans and body manacles. Many punks, particularly on the grassroots level, wear ordinary casual clothing such as t-shirt and jeans. If punks had a uniform, the movement would cease to exist because its essence is individuality.

It is really punk to exhibit anti-fashion statements. For example, Mark E. Smith (The Fall) usually wears on stage the kind of clothes that customers of Ladbrokes might wear while placing their bets on racehorses. Smith knows he is a genius, so his focus is where it should be – on his musicianship, rather than promoting designer clothes. Says Smith, *"I don't get off on wearing clothes… I don't go into clothes shops."*[53]

Poly Styrene (Marian Joan Elliott), vocalist of X-Ray Spex, defied music industry conventions by wearing prominent braces on her teeth on stage while screaming *"Oh Bondage, Up Yours!"*[46] Later she literally became a 'punk monk' by shaving her head, advocating ethical consumerism and joining the Hare Krishna movement.

Poly Styrene, daughter of dispossessed Somalian aristocrat, claims her epiphany occurred after a concert in Doncaster when she witnessed a Day-glo UFO. Says Poly, *"It was a bright ball of luminous pink, made of energy – like a fireball. Everyone else thought I'd lost the plot"*.[58]

The UK punk rock industry, however, was spearheaded by the fashion designer Vivienne Westwood and promoter Malcolm McLaren. The Sex Pistols were clotheshorses for Westwood's designer punk outfits which were retailed from the partners' *Sex* boutique on London's Fulham Road. Westwood's garments, which used swastikas, safety pins and sex-industry lingerie, were designed to shock people … and shock, they did.

Punks have a propensity for being tricksters and jokers, and some punks use visual imagery to enhance this theme. For example, Zal Clemenson, rock guitarist for SAHB (The Sensational Alex Harvey Band) and Nazareth dressed up as a joker on stage. Also Captain Sensible used comic imagery of The Fool to generate some fun.

32

"It's different for Jews somehow. I'd like to see a passionate film between the two ugliest people in the world... when I say "ugly", I don't mean rough-looking, I mean HIDEOUS."
- The Stranglers[61]

Ideally punks have no rules or rigid formulae for dress etiquette. They wear whatever suits them or what they feel comfortable wearing; not what they are expected to wear!

Urgency

The spirit of punk is furiously urgent and angst-ridden.

The Clash and The Sex Pistols are forerunners of compelling punk rock anthems. A sense of critical desperation is embraced by The Pistols' *Anarchy in the UK and Problems*; and also The Clashes' *London Calling* and *What's my Name?*

The lyrics of *London Calling* resonate with imminent global catastrophe. Here is the chorus:

"The Ice Age is coming; the sun's zooming in;
Meltdown expected; the wheat is growing thin;
Engines stop running, but I have no fear
'cause London is drowning and I live by the river."
- The Clash

Many punks live in the present moment without any plans for the future (with or without Buddhist intent). The pain of sudden trauma can smash to smithereens any cherished dreams of the future. Also punks living in perpetual danger focus on survival, one day at a time. As John Lennon says, *"Life is what happens to you while you're busy making other plans."*[41]

Several prolific punk rock icons shot to fame like shooting stars and later self-destructed in a blazing trail. Notable examples are Ian Curtis (Joy Division), Sid Vicious (The Sex Pistols), James Honeyman-Scott and Pete Farndon (The Pretenders) and Ricky Wilson (The B52s).

Two band members of The Pretenders (mentioned in the previous paragraph) died of drug overdoses. The Pretenders reflected urgency in their speedy song *Tattooed Love Boys* with commanding vocals by the sexually provocative Chrissie Hynde.[42]

The urgency of punk is the blade that lacerates the silk yarn of complacency. *London Calling* is an imperative harbinger of impending global destruction. The calendar of the ancient Mayan civilization draws to a close in December 2012 and many *"light-workers"* interpret this as the end of global capitalism. It may be Armageddon, but there are other problems much closer to home – the problem is you![44]

Outsiders

Punks are outsiders; and alienation, like charity, always begins at home.

Anyone, regardless of their class, education or family upbringing, is an outsider if they have been abandoned, rejected or otherwise branded "Black Sheep" by their parents. The ultimate outsider is spurned by their parents …

tossed away like garbage or reject goods … a psychological foundation for a life of broken relationships, fragmented career and low self-esteem. Everything else follows.

The working class is not the sole incubator of outsiders, black sheep and orphans. The great non-conformist genius John Lennon was raised by his aunt in an upper-middle class area of Liverpool. Lennon was dumped by his father, Fred Lennon, and later visited by him after his superstardom. John Lennon said, *"I showed him the door … I wasn't having him in the house"*.[38] Respect.

The widespread belief that punk is the exclusive domain of the working class is a myth. Of course it's cool or even fashionable to be a working class punk. The romantic ideal of a *"rags to riches"* punk rocker is irresistibly attractive publicity. Many middle class rebels, such as Tom Verlaine (Television), Lou Reed (Velvet Underground), Julian Casablancas (The Strokes), John Lennon (The Beatles) and Joe Strummer (The Clash) prefer to be identified as working class musicians. It's not cool to be a middle class rebel.

Mary Harron, author of *"Facing The Music"*, describes punk rock musicians as *"middle class children dressing up in a fantasy of proletarian aggression and lying desperately about their backgrounds"*. Prodigal son, Joe Strummer (The Clash) was an adept perception manager and publicist who denied his background.

Working class children are not always less comfortable economically than kids from middle class families. The anarchist author George Orwell complained of being used as *"scholarship fodder"*[36] by his private boarding school

35

because his lower-middle class parents could not afford to pay his school fees. Orwell was humiliated, treated as a lower class pupil by his compatriots and schoolmasters, and driven to study harder to justify his pauper's scholarship. George Orwell was a real outsider.

Three middle class promoter-presenters were the key UK pillars which supported the UK punk rock scene. They were Granada TV presenter Tony Wilson, BBC deejay John Peel, and Malcolm McLaren. Both John Peel and Tony Wilson always had security of a day job whereas the entrepreneurial McLaren - puppeteer of The Sex Pistols - played with his Jewish family wealth.

The penalty for being tolerated as a middle class punk outsider is either ridicule or vilification. John Peel was called a "c**t at festivals; Tony Wilson was known as *"a prat"*; and McLaren faced the anti-Semitic elements incorrectly associated with punk.

There is so much bitter resentment towards middle class artists. Artists should be judged on merit, and not according to the circumstances they were born into (which they had no control over). New York post-punk band, The Strokes, was slated for being a band of "spoiled rich kids"[37] with *"a spirit of revenge that festers in the weak, prompting them to seek vengeance against the strong, the noble and the talented"*.[39] Even though most members of The Strokes attended the Dwight School *"for rich fuck-ups"*, they have musical talent worthy of recognition. Thus The Strokes became outsiders in the indie music industry.

The widespread offensive against middle class non-conformist musicians has manifested in PR manipulation.

Punk or non-conformist musicians manipulate their family history to *"fit in"* with the standard industry profile. Points are scored for childhood poverty, criminal records and evidence of juvenile delinquency. Joe Strummer, for example, created his outlaw image by living in a London squat and bagging convictions for petty misdemeanors. John Lennon also modeled himself as a working class hero and even wrote a song about his romantic self-image.[40] Lennon's PR-manipulation caused resentment by the other Beatles who were genuine heroes from the working class.

Joe Strummer and his brother David were outsiders; both men were estranged from their parents. David committed suicide at the age of nineteen during his depression. Soon after David's death Joe changed his identity to Woody. Joe survived his dysfunctional middle class family by hiding his feelings of sadness and instead developing a tough exterior. Boarding school enabled Joe to cope with *"deep feelings of abandonment"* and to even deny the existence of his parents.[45]

Freedom

Nirvana's Curt Kobain once said, *"Punk is freedom."*

"La Poloma" may be the most recorded song in history, with versions in Cuba, Mexico, Hawaii, Romania, Germany, Spain and Tanzania.[62] *"Paloma"* is a Spanish girl's name which derives from the Latin word, *"Palumba"* meaning Dove, a Christian symbol for the Holy Ghost or spiritual liberation.[63] The Spanish composer, Sebastian Iradier (later, Yradier) wrote the song after visiting Cuba between 1861 and 1863. Iradier died in obscurity before the song became popular. Interestingly, *La Paloma Ha-*

37

banera was used for Georges Bizet's French opera Carmen, which was adapted later by punk promoter Malcolm McLaren for his album, *Fans*, in 1984.[64]

Chaos

The spirit of punk is chaotic.

Punk rock characterizes chaos on and off-stage by the musicians and fans alike. Mark E. Smith (The Fall) physically assaulted his musicians during a gig in New York. Smith expresses atrophy in unique forms of presentation art such as mumbling lyrics in monotone while reading from loose scraps of paper.

Tina Weymouth (Talking Heads and Tom Tom Club) commented about post-punk dance band Happy Mondays, *"I grew up in New York in the Seventies, and I've seen a lot of people who live life on the edge, but I've never before seen a group of people who had no idea where the edge is."*[50]

Meanwhile the punk rock audience is pogo-ing, spitting and throwing themselves at each other. The ambiance is ideally in a dark basement set in a cloud of smoke with the rancid odor of beer, sweat, urine and smoke. The phenomenon of spitting during punk rock gigs was introduced by The Damned who provoked their audience by spitting at them.[69] However some punk bands – notably The Clash - hated being showered with saliva.

The B52s - the quirky new wave party band from Georgia - expresses chaos in their lyrics.[51]

"Who's to blame when situations degenerate?
Disgusting things you'd never anticipate…
People get sick all over the place
You know, they could ruin your name!"
- The B52s

The Clashes' aggressive *"White Riot"* incited fans to destroy the seats at the Rainbow. The White Riot tour cost the band one quarter of their advance from their record company CBS.[67] Critics of The Clash interpreted the song as fascist, though the band refuted the accusation strongly.

"We're anti-fascist, anti-racist, and pro-creative"
- Joe Strummer[68]

Children at Heart

Many punks are children at heart. But let's remember that children have the ability to live in the present moment, while most adults have been conditioned to worry about past events or concerns about the future. What future? There is no future!

There is evidence that infants are born with the fundamental qualities of a genius; later, education changes all that … but the ethos of punk helps us regain our empowering qualities (of genius).

John Peel was called *"a perpetual adolescent"* meaning that he never *"grew up"* in the conventional way. For many people, *"growing up"* means compromising or even trashing their ideals; for others, it means reluctantly trying to fit into society like round pegs in square holes; or relinquishing coveted dreams.

Shedding Light on our Shadow

Punks and shamans are masters of shedding light on our dark stuff, labeled by psychologist Carl Gustav Jung as *The Shadow*. Modernity conditions us to express our positive qualities and achievements, while denying characteristics which may be deemed negative by society at large.

We are, after all, still animals with an urge to eat, drink, sleep and f**k. In between the four afore-mentioned pastimes, many of us lie and cheat, duck and dive, control and manipulate people and systems - just to survive in the rat-race.

Punks love to highlight illusions, hypocrisy, injustice and anything which authorities attempt to hide. Punk rock lyrics tend, therefore, to elicit emotive response from the audience. But some punk rock is almost pure art – free of political statements - like the band, Talking Heads for example.

Punk poet, John Cooper-Clarke from Salford, is a dour example of an artist shedding light on the societal murky waters which lie stagnant underneath the colorful lotus flower.

Wholism

Yes Men enhance their careers through progressive specialization; and inevitably experience tunnel vision. Punks prefer to see the wider picture and usually adopt the *"Jack of all Trades"* approach.

Punks are elusive, and like a bead of quicksilver, impossible to pin down. Maybe tomorrow they may express different personas on the other side of the planet. This is the spirit of freedom.

There are nine levels in the hierarchy of scale: zero, the void; 1, the atom, 2, the cell; 3, the organism; 4, the family; 5, the community; 6, the planet; 7, the solar system; 8, the Galaxy; 9, the Universe; and 10, The Source.

Shamans traverse all levels of scale for the benefit of their tribal community (the fifth level of scale). Most punks work on the level of community as well; whereas specialists operate at the fourth level, family.

Sexuality

The essence of punk is asexual; and quantity of sexual encounters presides over quality, with no holes barred.

If practitioners of white tantra place sexual union on top of a pedestal, punks debase sex and placing it underneath. Instead of a sacred fusion of yin and yang energies, sex is positioned by punks as *"two minutes of squelching."*[55] Perhaps sex is given similar importance to, *"a quick fag (cigarette) break"*.

Punks are not romantic. According to the Mancunian legend captured on the film, *"24 Hour Party People"*[56], Tony Wilson had sex with prostitutes in a car during a Joy Divison gig; and later Howard Devoto (The Buzzcocks) engaged in *"full penetrative sex"* with Wilson's first wife, Lyndsay (Shirley Henderson) in the public toilets.

The mystique is torn out of sensuality when the punk's fetish gear is ripped and covered in vomit. The sexual act is mechanical; and the drug-induced carnal opportunity is handed around glibly like a packet of Wrigley's chewing gum.

Punk could be perceived as androgynous. David Bowie, who collaborated with his friend Iggy Pop, created the sexually unidentifiable personas, Aladin Sane and Ziggy Stardust. Aladin Sane (or a lad insane) is believed to have been inspired by Bowie's schizophrenic brother.[57]

Johnny Morrissey of The Smiths has been classified as *"prophet of the fourth sex"* for living the saintly life of a celibate vegetarian. Morrissey admitted, *"I'm just simply inches away from a monastery and I feel that perhaps if I wasn't doing this, that I probably would be in one."*[65]

Conclusion

There exists *"authentic punk"* and *"pseudo-punk"*. The essence of authentic punk is buried underneath the façade of pseudo-punk.

Authentic punk is a state of mind and being which bypasses social class and economy. Punks are outsiders and there are plenty of middle class punks out there (without colorful tattoos or Mohawk hairstyles) whether they lie about their background or not.

The main characteristics of authentic punk are uniqueness, capacity for reinvention, non-conformity (rather than outright rebellion), shedding light on The Shadow, and resourcefulness. The goal of authentic punk is freedom of creative expression; and their enemies are found in limiting restrictions and standards, interfering control and manipulation, and outdated rigid or unjust systems.

Pseudo punk is driven by nihilism, commercial exploitation, insanity, political extremism, criminality and juvenile delinquency. Pseudo-punk takes but does not give anything positive back; and is characterized by immaturity, emotional reaction, rebelliousness and brazen provocation with intent to offend or cause harm.

PART TWO: PUNK PHILOSOPHY by Crispin Sartwell[70]

Perhaps you're wondering what could be meant by the *"philosophy"* of punk music. But before I elucidate that deeply profound matter, allow me to briefly sketch in the history of the form for you.

Though punk had a variety of important antecedents, such as the Velvet Underground and Iggy Pop, it's generally agreed that the form was invented in 1975 in NYC by the Ramones with the aid of somewhat related acts such as Blondie and the Talking Heads. At the time, punk was received as the acme of primitivism, and the people who made and consumed it were widely regarded as dolts. The Ramones themselves did little to dispel this impression, performing songs such as *"Teenage Lobotomy"* and *"Now I Wanna Sniff Some Glue."* What most people seemed to hear at the time was fast and furious noise, dedicated to nihilism as a strategy for personal growth. The style was dismissed as trivial at best, and deeply stupid and offensive to decency at worst.

But in fact the Ramones were (a) jokers, and (b) rock archivists. The style they played is best considered neo-classical, while the musical context into which they emerged was rank and rococo. The horrors of mid-seventies popular music included *"art rock"* - the kind of pseudo-profound conceptual claptrap dished out by Yes or Emerson, Lake, and Palmer, in which former conservatory students, or young men who simply aspired to be conservatory students, played real real fast though meaninglessly and inexpressively under lyrics inspired by a superficial reading of Jules Verne.

It was indeed a sad time. The other pole was glossy California rock made by bands such as Fleetwood Mac and the Eagles: utterly slick, though catchy, and dedicated to the idea that cocaine and orgies were the ultimate agents of human liberation. This conceit was exploded some years later as the artists involved declined with awesome rapidity and bounced in and out of rehab, a trend that continues until this very day, as Stevie Nicks declines into an unseemly dotage.

Something, as you can deduce, had to be done, and the Ramones did it. They were a rock band ultimately in the style of the Rolling Stones, interested in finding at the heart of the form its essential gesture, the one thing without which it would lose its soul. They were familiar with every simple and crystalline rock style, from rhythm and blues to girl group to surf and bubblegum, and they recreated them all with an ironic precision that is as close to perfection as rock music has ever come.

The Ramones toured England in 1976, and folks who would soon become the Clash and the Sex Pistols showed up at the shows and were forever changed. But by 1980, the initial momentum had been squandered. Though the Clash pressed on, the Pistols exploded. The Talking Heads became artistes, and Blondie became a pop act. The Ramones, believe it or not, continued to deepen and improve, a trend that persisted even after Joey's death in 2001 with the release of his lovely punk solo album.

In 1979 and 80, the form received a fresh dose of ferocity in LA and DC from bands like the Germs and the Teen Idles, who invented hardcore. Soon there was a blossoming scene of ferocious noise on both coasts, featuring

LA bands like the Circle Jerks and Black Flag, and DC types such as Minor Threat and the Faith. The LA bands were more or less dedicated to decadence, but in DC, as befits the town, the bands soon became extremely earnest and political, and merged with activist organizations. The east-coast scene soon developed toward *"emo"* and *"grunge,"* and gave Dave Grohl to Nirvana and the Foo Fighters, and Fugazi to everyone. By the early nineties, the *"alternative"* punk revival was in full swing in Seattle, then everywhere. And by the mid-nineties a revival of straight-up classic punk had emerged, spearheaded on the pop charts by Green Day, and nurtured by a burbling underground of labels and acts who loved the Ramones above all things. Check out some Screeching Weasel, for example. The current state of play is that there are probably more punk rock bands than there have ever been, and the dominant pop rock of the current era - Blink 182, Sum 41, even No Doubt - comes from and pays homage to punk music. Hardcore is now absolutely global; in fact, the most vital scenes seem to be in Scandinavia and Japan.

Now punk is a lot of different things and it supports a lot of different ideas or postures toward the world. There is of course right-wing or neo-fascist skinhead punk, or at least there used to be, especially in NYC. Bands like the Cro-Mags and Agnostic Front weren't or aren't necessarily Nazis, but violent thugs undeniably gravitated toward their shows and records. But then of course there is also far-left punk, represented by bands such as the Clash, Dead Kennedys or Millions of Dead Cops. Those were classic backintheday hardcore acts, though Jello Biafra is still around, mutating into a Noam Chomsky-type intellectual. And there is a huge, active left-wing punk scene now, especially including the band Anti-Flag, which is a good band and delivers leftist lectures over Clash-type thrash.

46

But I guess the paradigm for me is the DC hardcore scene; I was eighteen in '76, in NW DC: Minor Threat, obviously; Rites of Spring; G.I., Faith, and so on: the bands that started and the people who continued Dischord Records, especially Ian Mackaye. The basic idea of Dischord Records is that first of all, it stays outside the purview of the major corporate record labels: it is fiercely independent. This is also the approach of Jello's label in San Francisco: Alternative Tentacles. Ian Mackaye's band Fugazi was in the Spin top 50 most influential rock bands, as well it should have been; in some ways it invented *"emo"* and *"alternative."* But the sales of Fugazi's albums are relatively modest compared to, say, Creed, or Stone Temple Pilots, bands that are infinitely less interesting. That's because there's no big promo push, and believe it or not there's no merchandise: no Fugazi t-shirts or bumper stickers, except bootlegged things. Dischord essentially sells disks at cost: maybe 10 bucks for a full-length cd. It costs five or six bucks to get into a Fugazi show, if you can believe that. They cover their expenses, pay themselves a decent salary, but they're not out here getting rich as motherfuckers.

Dischord is conceived as a library of DC punk music; they don't have A&R people out trying to recruit hot young talent. And they've managed to hold onto their values for twenty years. Mackaye says things like this: *"It's not that I'm out to smash the state. I'm just interested in building my own damn state."* He's not interested in tearing down the system; he's interested in building his own little system, or his own zone within the system where he can live and create the way he wants to. The punk world, once you cut through the rankest pop of Blink or Sum, is like this; go get a copy of Maximum RocknRoll and you'll see that there are hundreds of bands and dozens of labels who are operating entirely outside the artistic and spiritual Sahara of major-label music.

I think this exactly the right sort of politics. And now let me do something that may strike y'all as a bit absurd; I'm going to trace some historical antecedents to Mackaye's approach and the approach of what we might think of as the left-anarchist punk world.

We might start out in the early sixteenth century with Martin Luther and the Protestant Reformation. Of course Luther was no anarchist; in fact he was a German nationalist. But his objection to the Catholic church accused it of insane greed and acquisitiveness, and accused it above all of coming between each person and God. Finally, the scene of religious experience and interpretation for Luther was each individual believer. Early in his rebellion against the Catholic church, he wrote: *"I will tell you straight what I think. I am a Christian theologian; and I am bound, not only to assert, but to defend the truth with my blood and my death. I want to believe freely and be the slave to the authority of no one, whether council, university, or pope."* Every believer was, for Luther, a minister of Christ: *"All of us who have been baptized are priests without distinction."* And the church had to be conceived of as a community of believers, answerable above all to their own consciences, rather than as an authoritarian hierarchy. This a fundamental stroke for what punks call DIY. Make your own fucking records. Set up your own fucking tours. Achieve your own fucking relation to God, if any.

It's a familiar point that the Reformation leads fairly directly to the enlightenment, where thinkers like Hume and Voltaire became atheists, more or less. That's where their exercise of independent conscience took them. And this whole deal leads to the call for political freedom, for democracy as expressed in the American and French revolutions. And the final flowering of this attitude is political anarchism: the call for the total elimination of authoritarian structures, religious, political, and economic. And though there are hints of anarchism from ancient philosophy (for example in the Tao Te Ching), the invention of modern anarchism must in my view be ascribed fundamentally to the American Josiah Warren and the Frenchman Pierre-Joseph Proudhon. And there is a profound anti-authoritarian tradition in America that proceeds from Warren to Emerson and Thoreau, to Emma Goldman and Alexander Berkman, Albert Jay Nock and H.L. Mencken, Abbie Hoffman and Noam Chomsky, Ian Mackaye and Jello Biafra.

Let me discuss Josiah Warren's work in a little more depth, because I think that you'll find there more or less the entire punk thing enunciated starting in the 1820s. Warren was initially a follower of Robert Owen, and participated in Warren's utopian socialist community of New Harmony. But that community was by and large a failure, and Warren attributed that failure to the authoritarian structure that began in the cult of Owen's personality. He dedicated the rest of his life to establishing his own utopian businesses and communities, and the shocking thing (considering that Warren is almost forgotten) is that communities such as *"Trialville"* were extremely successful. 80 quarter-acre lots were sold at fifteen bucks a pop, and the economy was put on what we would think of as a barter footing: labor-for-labor exchange was the means by which the community was developed. Warren tried intentionally to shield the community from publicity, refusing even to disclose its location in Ohio. In fact, it was in part publicity that doomed many of the utopian experiments in 19th century America, including Warren's own later attempt: Modern Times, on Long Island, which through no fault of Warren's got processed through the NY press and various pr entrepreneurs.

Warren's work, both practical and theoretical, was dedicated to two principles: the sovereignty of the individual and the cost limit of price. On the first he asserted that all people, black and white, male and female - even children - have the right to dispose of their own persons as they see fit, unless they violate the liberty of others to do likewise. And since governmental, religious, and corporate structures invariably proceeded by violation of the sovereignty of the individual, they were inherently evil, evil at their very conception. He wrote this: *"Experience has proved, that power cannot be delegated to rulers of state and nations, in sufficient quantities for the management of business, without its becoming an indefinite quantity, and in this indefiniteness have mankind been cheated out of their legitimate liberty."*

Concerning the cost limit of price, his view was this: most of the evil and poverty in the world is caused by the greed for profit and the imposition of interest on the use of funds. Warren, well before Marx, had the labor theory of value down cold: what a thing was worth was what labor went into it, and the labor of a lawyer was no more inherently valuable than that of a laborer. As he puts it in his almost unknown classic *"Equitable Commerce"*:

Cost being made the limit of price, would give to a washerwoman a greater income than the importer of for-

50

eign goods - that this would upset the whole of the present system of national trade - stop all wars arising out of the profits of trade, and demolish all tariffs, duties, and all systems of policy that give rise to them - would abolish all distinctions between rich and poor - would enable every one to consume as much as he produced, and, consequently, prevent any one from living at the cost of another, without his of her consent.

Things should be sold for exactly what they cost to produce and sell: the raw materials and the time that went into their making and marketing. If a community or a business could commit itself to that principle, then it could undersell communities and businesses based on the profit motive, and so in the long run could succeed and spread, slowly replacing an economy based on profit to one based on labor, without violence or constraint.

Warren actually established an extremely successful business along these lines: the Cincinnati time store. He sold staple fabrics and foods, and charged according to the time that went into their making. And he accepted *"labor notes"* as currency: notes that pledged a quantity of labor in exchange for goods purchased. He hoped that a labor currency could eventually replace currency based on gold and silver, so that almost everyone could have sufficient money because everyone has fundamentally the same quantity of time at their disposal. The details of how this would work are of course complex, and I can't really enter into them here; suffice it to say that Warren showed that the practical application of his principles was possible.

This is, it seems to me, a quintessentially American philosophy, and it is totally opposed, for example, to the authoritarian socialism of Marx, Lenin, or Mao. It is exactly the opposite of a command economy. And yet it is also not some laissez-faire, dog-eat-dog corporate capitalism. The economy it envisions is radically decentralized and egalitarian. Perhaps it is also naively idealistic, but it can be tried practically, and essentially Dischord and Alternative Tentacles are attempts to put something like this into practice.

A more recent version of a Warren-type approach is the TAZ: *Temporary Autonomous Zone*. The book of that title, which is available for free online, or cheaply from the anarchist publishing collective autonomedia, is, I think, the most important political tract of the last few decades. I personally would like to tear down the INS or the IRS or the Sony corporation, brick by fucking brick, to erase them hard drive by hard drive. But I'm not able to, you see? The systems that we have created or that have been created at us are far too huge, powerful, and unresponsive to be resisted by direct attack. And these systems are getting bigger and more centralized all the time; note the unification of the European currencies, for example, or the way the United Nations seeks to act as a world government, or the reach of Nike corporation around the world and its ever-growing implication in economic exploitation, or the vicious monopoly of bad software achieved by Bill Gates.

Here's a sample of Bey's book:

No, listen, what happened was this: they lied to you, sold you ideas of good & evil, gave you distrust of your body & shame for your prophethood of chaos, invented words of disgust for your molecular love, mesmerized you with inattention, bored you with civilization & all its usurious emotions.

There is no becoming, no revolution, no struggle, no path; already you're the monarch of your own skin--your inviolable freedom waits to be completed only by the love of other monarchs: a politics of dream, urgent as the blueness of sky.

To shed all the illusory rights & hesitations of history demands the economy of some legendary Stone Age--shamans not priests, bards not lords, hunters not police, gatherers of paleolithic laziness, gentle as blood, going naked for a sign or painted as birds, poised on the wave of explicit presence, the clockless nowever.

Agents of chaos cast burning glances at anything or anyone capable of bearing witness to their condition, their fever of lux et voluptas. I am awake only in what I love & desire to the point of terror--everything else is just shrouded furniture, quotidian anaesthesia, shit-for-brains, subreptilian ennui of totalitarian regimes, banal censorship & useless pain.

But what you and I might be able to do is find or create little zones outside these systems, pirate utopias that last a few hours or a few years or a few decades, tiny places where you go unnoticed or unconstrained by the bigger systems, like Warren's Trialville. There are still gaps in the universal surveillance, still corners where you can hide and hatch your diabolical schemes, places on the internet where you can say whatever you damn please and AOL or the Justice Department haven't figured out quite how to shut you up.

Of course, maybe we'd prefer a real revolution. But it is extremely unlikely, given that corporate capitalism has

53

managed to give most Americans a stake in the status quo. But even if a real revolution was possible, there are a few things wrong with real revolutions, as history makes all too obvious. Often they end up with *"the terror."* Anarchists helped overthrow the Czar, then were executed en masse by Lenin. The cultural revolution and the Killing Fields are examples of what can happen when your basic leftists take over, with their little red books and their automatic weapons . The systematic revolution supposes a systematic ideology, and the systematic ideology always holds within it the seeds of slaughter.

Well the TAZ makes a revolution, a tiny revolution, without ideology. The idea is just to carve out a place where people can do what they want. That, I think, is the only revolution worth having, and it was exactly the sort of revolution proposed by Thoreau, say, and put into actual operation by Warren and Mackaye. It's a revolution that's actually being made all the time by punks, freaks, druggies, weirdos, and lovers. I do not recognize the right of anyone to control my words or my actions, and I claim the right to resist in any way I deem appropriate. And I am willing to extend the same courtesy to you, to recognize that you are the sovereign of yourself. If I start with that, then I can't also design society by some ideal structure, because ideal structures are just more or less creative oppressions. I just have to let go and see what happens. That's the only politics that isn't worse than what it seeks to replace.

And that's what I call punk philosophy: DIY; the cost limit of price; the sovereignty of the person over themselves; the temporary autonomous zone, not to mention zine. We see this in many other of the most vital areas of the culture. For example, in hip hop, particularly in graffiti art. The tag is both an intra-sub-cultural form of communication and a subversion of public space. You might find similar things if you hit the big biker's convention in Daytona, or start hanging out at skate parks. These are the only sorts of places where the culture is not dead; as Deleuze and Guattari would put it, these minor languages and minor threats are the places where the culture becomes; they are at once the flowering and the undermining of American culture. Make your own art, your own love, your own truth, and find a place where you can do that. If you can't find a place like that, start trying to carve one out; make your own island nation of jesters and fools and fops. For God's sake ditch Shakira and make your own music. Get on the web and publish your own fucked-up writing and see whether someone reads it.

CHAPTER 2

THE WORLD OF TRICKSTERS

The purpose of this chapter is to show the association between the mythological trickster and both punks and shamans.

The Trickster is probably the most entertaining of archetypal deities and folklore heroes. Versions of the Trickster originate from myths and folk stories in the tribal cultures of North and South America, Asia, Africa and Scandinavia – wherever indigenous shamans have lived.

The Trickster is a magician, alchemist, trouble-maker and rule-breaker; also a fertile and lustful fornicator with the ability to change sex and shape-shift between human and animal form. This flamboyant character is the cheat, provocateur, clown and joker, always overturning order and propagating chaos. The Trickster meets perfectionists during their most scary nightmares. However, the Trickster also serves humanity by shedding light upon its shady illusions, injustices and outdated conventions.

Carl Jung described the trickster archetype as belonging to the collective shadow and typically defying societal expectations. Mythologist Joseph Campbell refers to the trickster as *"the giver of boons, the fire bringer and teacher of humanity."* Like Inspector Jacques Clouseau of Pink Panther fame, the genius of the Trickster is often veiled by a façade of foolishness.

The archetypal trickster is as provocative as he is potent. Embodied in Loony Tune's Coyote, he's sly, sneaky, manipulative, while causing all sorts of trouble. He stole Water Monster's baby, brought on the great flood, and is known for being a glutton, a liar, a lecher, and a cheat. Trickster even hurled the stars into the night sky, recognized the value of death as a necessary evil, and stole fire from Black God to relieve the suffering of First Man and First Woman.[17]

Punks on the other hand are popularly portrayed as colorful jokers who flout social conventions and highlight society's quagmire. Punks and tricksters alike are rule-breakers, self-re-inventers, masters of disguise, uncompromising *"Jack-of-all-Trades"*; and they love to question – and poke fun at - authority.

Georg Feuerstein describes the Trickster, thus[1]:

"The trickster, who is usually male, belongs to the realm of tribal religion and mythology. He is either an archetypal demigod or superhuman hero. He is a being who is very clever but unprincipled, delighting in the irrational. There is an element of malice in many trickster figures, though they are never entirely demonic. They are out to best their adversaries and spare no cunning to achieve their goal. As part of their duplicity, they often pretend to be stupid. They are generally depicted as merciless, cruel visitors. At times, the trickster is killed in a fight, but it is always understood that he can come back to life."

Many aspects of the trickster are innate to punk, particularly his crudity and penchant for reinvention. The trickster knows no shame because he does not delineate between right and wrong. The trickster is a rampant hedonist with an insatiable appetite for pleasure. If monks try to minimize their "attachments", trickster punks maximize sensory attachment.

Tricksters are often described as nomadic travellers who use their cunning to dupe their victims along their way in order to gratify their insatiable appetite for food, drink and sex. Trickster loves to unleash shenanigans upon unsuspecting victims.

On the positive side, tricksters bring wisdom and culture to society by highlighting our shadow – the dark stuff we deny – as punk rockers do. Ultimately tricksters bring balance to the world by being audacious harbingers of bad news – anything from injustice to global warming.

Shaman-tricksters, commonly associated with hunting, are depicted in cave paintings dating back to 16,000 BC. Therefore the Shaman-Trickster archetype is older than the Hero, Warrior or King archetypes.[6] Shamans are known for communicating with animals, whereas tricksters have a tendency to shape-shift into different animal forms as a means of disguise.

Sexuality

Powerful sexual libido and unbridled lust are common characteristics amongst tricksters. Franchot Ballinger reveals that the Yurok trickster, Wohpekumeu, has such strong sexual potency that his glance alone impregnates women[10]. Joe Strummer (The Clash) admitted that although he would never steal money from a friend, he might steal his girlfriend.[11]

Tricksters are not only exceptionally fertile, they tend

to have massive penises – and they use them *"willy-nilly"* with brash prowess. The North American trickster, Nana-bush[12], is believed to be so well endowed that he carried his penis in a box on his back. Sexually, tricksters are un-restrained, vulgar and slave to their base instincts.

The trickster's sexuality is essentially masculine, though there are occasional folk tales of female tricksters. Females tend to use their sexual appeal to manipulate men, whereas male tricksters use their cunning and resourceful-ness to ensnare their target using a complex maze of barbed words. Tricksters, therefore, are nearly always male.

Female tricksters tend to be vamps and harlots, skilled in the art of manipulating men. An example of a female trickster is the archetypal Actress from Thailand, an adept ensnarer of men. Phil Nicks's definition of the *Actress* fol-lows[15]:

The Actress is unbelievably charming and truly gifted. She is whatever you want her to be; but every flutter of her eyelids and each radiating smile - rehearsed a zillion times - are part of "the act" (and therefore billable).

The Actress will have you in her pocket, along with your wallet and house keys. She will have you dancing – to her tune – around her little brown finger.

The Oscar-nominated starlet from Issan[13] is the ul-timate Party Girl. The Actress is the Siamese clone of Courtney Love[14]; she always makes her partner believe he's in nirvana.

Her heart – if she has one – is microscopic, impervi-ous and as dark as her complexion. Her partner will never

*know who she really is – but he will observe her athletic
ability when his money runs out.*

Phil Nicks wrote the book, *Love Entrepreneurs* [16], about
the female trickster-predators of the Land of Smiles.

According to South American folklore, trickster Fox
is a wily fornicator and Jaguar is dangerously stupid. On
one occasion, Fox tied a bladder full of stones to Jaguar's
tail and screamed, *"Wake up! Hunters are coming after
you!"* Immediately Jaguar drags the stones away into the
distance while Fox has sex with Jaguar's wife.[33]

The lustful trickster Tokwah is known for indiscrimi-
nate serial fornication along his travels. Tokwah gave semen to man to enable procreation. He did so by piercing
a toad's anus with a thorn, causing it to secrete a milky
fluid, and then daubed the liquid onto Man's penis. After
Tokwah's invention of spermatozoa, he introduced adultery, followed by crime of passion.[34]

The Trickster is Polytropic

Trickster is polytropic, which means *"turning many
ways"*, wily, versatile and *"much traveled"*. Trickster is
*"shifty as an octopus, coloring himself to fit his surround-
ings, putting on a fresh face for each man or woman he
meets, charming, disarming, and not to be trusted. (He
makes a good politician, especially in a democracy, where
many voters call for many faces.[2])"*

The Nordic trickster, Loki, sometimes appears as a
bird, but also as a flea, a horse or on other occasions, as fire.
So who is the real Loki? Does the trickster have his own

61

way, or does he just imitate others? Lewis Hyde concludes that the trickster has no unique way of his own, *"only the many ways of their shape-shifting skins and changing contexts.* [3]*"*

In the Chapter 3, *How Outsiders Love Asia*, there is evidence that a body of punk outsiders experience *"hopelessness and a tendency to lose touch with their true selves.*[4]*"* People who experience identity crisis and who have lost their own way are best suited to the task of self-reinvention. Since they are not centered in their true self, they fabricate false ways and therefore appear to the world as chameleons.

Rob Gretton, manager of punk band Joy Division, told Tony Wilson, the director of Factory Records that he was aware of Wilson's real identity. Wilson intimated that curiosity had the better of him, indirectly questioning his own identity. The manager looked Wilson straight into his eyes and said, *"You're a c**t, mate!"*[19]

Trickster is Entertaining

Trickster is a flamboyant jester who enjoys playing with words - and especially ambiguity - and shocking his audience with the punch line. William Shakespeare created The Fool – a court jester in his play, King Lear - to incite amusement amongst the audience.

The punk rock band, The Sensational Alex Harvey Band (SAHB), employed Zal Cleminson as bass guitarist. Ex-Nazareth Cleminson always played SAHB wearing his customary joker outfit. And front man Alex Harvey reenacted the crucifixion of Christ onstage -with a polystyrene cross attached to his back - to the lyric, *"I was framed!"*[5]

In one folk story the Nordic trickster Loki, entertained the guests at the wedding party of Skadi (the Snow-shoe Goddess) and Njord (the god with the beautiful feet). Loki made Skadi and others laugh by attaching the beard of a goat to his testicles.[22]

Tricksters are cunning magicians who master the art of timing; they are unpredictable, turning up (or failing to turn up) when least expected. Unpredictability is the ethos of punk. Mark E. Smith (The Fall), Malcolm McLaren (manager of the Sex Pistols) and Johnny Rotten (John Lydon, Sex Pistols) each demonstrate the art of unpredictability. Trickster Mark E Smith is not averse to fighting with fellow band members onstage; and the Sex Pistols cancelled their entire tour schedule without prior notice; and Wile E Coyote inevitably turns up when least expected.

As mentioned in the first chapter, Raymond Burns (Captain Sensible, politician and member of punk band, The Damned) is a good example of a colorful jester with the ability to simultaneously amuse, ridicule and communicate important issues. Tricksters never die; although they may fail in the short-term... later they will reinvent themselves under a new guise and a different name ... and it's impossible to keep track of their elusive antics...

Tony Wilson, director of Factory Records, is famous for signing a record deal with Joy Division with his own blood. Such dramatic behavior is true to punk tricksters. Later, when the record company (or cooperative) went bankrupt, the band (renamed New Order) lost money despite achieving hit singles in the record charts.
That's entertainment![18]

Trickster is a Rule-Breaker

The duplicitous trickster is an adept liar, cheat and rule-breaker. The trickster is universally perceived as a mischievous anti-hero without any sense of morality and no respect for manmade laws, rules, conventions, taboos and customs.

The trickster is ultimately free; and he has supernatural ability to survive his reckless misadventures. He is the enemy of authority, especially control freaks; and he has a penchant for poking fun at pomposity, pride and any form of illusion.

When Joe Strummer (The Clash) lived in Newport, before he sang with The 101ers, he wrote about wanting to lead a criminal lifestyle.[9] Strummer fantasized about being a cat burglar or a bank robber (like Ronnie Biggs who sang Frank Sinatra's *"My Way"* with The Sex Pistols). Later Strummer associated with Sex Pistols' Steve Jones, a former house-breaker; and deejay Robin Banks who was previously convicted of armed robbery.

Chaos and Disorder

The energy of the trickster is chaotic. The trickster typically waits for signs of distinction, prestige, pride and pretension before unleashing catastrophic devastation and ultimately downfall. *"He can reduce to a shambles the most carefully ordered pattern of meaning, plan of action or contrived self-concept, as he especially resists being controlled, grounded or owned."[17]*

Winnebago Indians say that Earthmaker strived for structure, law and order throughout the world, so he established a lodge for each living species. Along came the Winnebago trickster known as Wakdjunkaga who let rip a massive fart which blew away the lodges and scattered the animals across the world. A single act of uncouth flatulence caused all our earthly troubles.

Perhaps the advent of punk rock was similar to Wakdjunkaga's fart. Indeed, radio deejay John Peel referred to punk as *"a welcome blast of foul air."* And punk rock is certainly chaotic.

Maui, the ugly Polynesian trickster God, went fishing with his brothers but they refused to give him bait. Unperturbed and resourceful as tricksters are, Maui attached his grandmother's jawbone to his fisherman's hook and cast it far out to sea. Shortly afterwards, Maui pulled up the Polynesian islands from the seabed. He also lassoed the sun in a noose, causing it to slow down its rotation around the galactic centre; thereby extending daytime.[21]

Trickster is Wily

Tricksters are cunning deviants, and ever vigilant of nebulous *"grey zones"* between outright white and white. Trickster delights in the exploitation of loopholes in the lay of the land.

Of course, Trickster applies his cunning for the endgame of feeding his belly or fulfilling his voracious sexual desires; but even when there is no meat or sex to be had, causing anguish to others is pleasurable.

In the following Apache story which originates from Texas, the trickster Rabbit deceives Coyote.[29]

In the middle of a field of watermelons, the farmer placed a stick figure covered with gum. One day Rabbit hit the farmer's trap and got stuck to it. Later Coyote found the ensnared rabbit and asked him what he was doing. Rabbit told Coyote, *"The farmer is angry with me because I would not eat watermelons with him, so he stuck me here. Shortly afterwards the farmer will return and force me to eat chicken with him."* The hungry Coyote told Rabbit how foolish he was, and that he would take his place. So Coyote pulled Rabbit away from the gum trap and adhered his body to the stick figure. When the farmer returned to his field of watermelons, he found Coyote and shot him full of holes.

In Greek mythology, when Hades, the god of the dead, came to claim the wily trickster Sisyphus, he brought handcuffs with him. Sisyphus displayed such enthusiasm for the novelty of handcuffs that he managed to persuade Hades to demonstrate their use on himself. And so it was that Sisyphus imprisoned the god of the dead in his own house. Sisyphus's act caused widespread chaos because nobody was able to die during Hades' imprisonment.[44]

Trickster is Childish

Tricksters are ever childish at heart and never compromise themselves by adapting their behavior to meet societal conventions. Trickster is driven by passionate desires rather than compulsion to win at someone else's game. Being a lonesome outsider facilitates Trickster's resistance to compromise.

Trickster, like Mr Bean, is mischievous and often malicious. Rowan Atkinson's Mr Bean delights in hurting his doting girlfriend's feelings. Once, Mr Bean presented his eager girlfriend with a jewelry box as a gift. When his excited girlfriend opened the presentation box she was mortified to discover it contained a hook which had purchased from a hardware store.

Punks and shamans don't grow up, settle down and fit in. Never.

Trickster is Amoral

Trickster has no sense of right or wrong, and therefore he satisfies his carnal desires with gusto and without shame. Society failed to condition Trickster's mind with any religious dogma, sense of morality or value system. So Trickster has no conscience and never abstains from fulfilling any passionate desire.

Shamans and punks are famous for their use of drugs. Shamans use drugs to enhance awareness of alternative dimensions; whereas punks enjoy *"mood enhancement"* for the hedonists' *"high"*. Both punks and shamans tend to use drugs shamelessly and without self-judgment.

Trickster is Foolish-Clumsy

Trickster is seemingly foolish and clumsy. In the story which follows, the Native American Winnebago trickster is genuinely stupid.

Trickster looked into the lake and there he saw several plums which whetted his appetite for food. Without a thought, he dived into the lake but he found nothing other than stones. He dived into the lake a second time and this time he hit his head on the bed of the lake. The impact caused Trickster to have concussion; so as he floated on the water, lying on his back, he was unconscious. When he regained consciousness he noticed a fruit-laden plum tree on the bank of the lake; and immediately he realized he had seen a reflection of the plums on the surface of the water. *"Oh, my!"* said Trickster, *"What a stupid fellow I must be! I should have recognized this. Indeed I have caused myself a great deal of pain."*[20]

Sometimes, however, Trickster's "mistakes" are actually premeditated stratagems to catch his prey off-guard. Detective Clouseau in *The Pink Panther* – acted by Peter Sellers, and recently by Steve Martin – is an appropriate example of a cunning trickster pretending to be foolish until after his prey has been ensnared.

Go-Between and In-Between

Trickster is a messenger and mediator between Earth and the spirit world. He has supernatural powers as a demigod, being part human and part God, enabling him to live unlimited lives.

Whereas Roadrunner Wile E. Coyote reemerges (in some form or other) after his demise, Mark E. Smith (The Fall) drawls the lyrics, *"I'm just in-between...uhh!"*[7]. Lewis Hyde describes Trickster as *"The God of The Crossroads"* due to trickster Eshu's introduction of the Yoruba divination system[8] for those wanting to know which way to turn next.

The Trickster, like the shaman, is a mediator between human beings and animals. He has magical powers to transform his human body into animal form. Trickster is a shamanic showman with a penchant for practical – and sometimes malicious - jokes.

Wile E Coyote (Loony Toons) is a popular comic trickster who influenced the punk movement. Other tricksters include David Bowie's androgynous personas known as *Ziggy Stardust* and *Aladin Sane* (A Lad Insane); the Joker in Batman; and Jim Carrey's representation of *The Mask*.

The Trickster archetype is dominant throughout the punk movement and shamanism. The link between tricksters and punk is clear. Myriad trickster tales involve The Sex Pistols and their manager Malcolm McLaren[23], and Mark E. Smith and his numerous ex band members[24]. A punk trickster worthy of note is Jello Biafra who fronted the Dead Kennedys.

Jello Biafra

Jello Biafra is the anti-brand name of Eric Reed Boucher, previously the singer-songwriter of far-left punk rock band the Dead Kennedys, spoken-word artist, *"Noam Chomsky-type intellectual"*[39], DIY record producer of outsider music, culture-jammer extraordinaire, political candidate for the Green Party, and outspoken trickster-provocateur with a penchant for absurdist media tactics. Many punks credit Biafra to be an anarchic genius.

Jello Biafra's name combines the brand name of the mal-nutritious sugary food, *Jell-O*, with the name of one of the world's impoverished nations. Therefore a trickster-style 'ad-buster' permeates the core of Biafra's public identity.

69

In 1978 Biafra responded to an advertisement by East Bay Ray, stating *"Guitarist wants to form punk band"* and together they formed the Dead Kennedys. Biafra was the band's vocalist who wrote most of the lyrics. The band's most controversial album, *Frankenchrist*, was the catalyst for Biafra's obscenity prosecution. Ultimately charges were dropped but the Dead Kennedys disbanded.

Biafra established the fiercely independent underground record label, Alternative Tentacles in 1979. The business is described by Alternativetentacles.com as *"most likely the longest lasting underground record label around"*. The label recorded punk rock bands, The Dead Kennedys, Butthole Surfers, D.O.A. to name a few, and political spoken word. Biafra describes his position in the 'disorganization' as 'absentee thoughtlord'.

The absentee thoughtlord has a knack for selecting quirky names for his bands, albums and songs. Biafra formed a four piece band called *Jello Biafra and the Axis of Merry Evildoers* (poking fun at President George Bush) and afterwards, *Jello Biafra and The Guantanamo School of Medicine*.[40]

Remember, tricksters have a knack of disseminating wisdom by poking fun at authority… well, in 1979 Biafra ran for mayor of San Francisco at the age of 21 using the *Jell-O* ad campaign slogan, *"There's always room for Jello."* Rumors abound that Biafra wrote his keynote speech on a napkin during a Pere Ubu concert. The political stuntman confused some voters by wearing a campaign t-shirt previously used by one of his rivals.

Biafra's mayoral manifesto included forcing businessmen to wear clown suits within city limits, and erecting statues of Harvey Milk's assassin, Dan White, throughout the city for the public to pelt with eggs and tomatoes. Political activist Biafra, who also wanted to legalize squatting in vacant buildings, ended up in fourth place (out of ten) with 3.79% of the vote.

Biafra was nominated as a candidate for the Green Party (for President of the United States) in 2000 and ended up in second place after Ralph Nader. Biafra's running mate was convicted cop-killer and Death Row inmate Mumia Abu-Jamal. The catchphrase of alternative media, *"Don't hate the media, be the media"* arose from Biafra's album, *Become the Media*.

Rascal Monks

There are plenty of rascal monks, crazy gurus and cult *"masters"* awaiting queues of eager middle class f**kups, outsiders, and broken down, disenchanted and emotionally vulnerable societal rejects. Victims and losers at the bottom of the economy tend to be served by their nation's welfare system, if any. It's more difficult for middle class rejects to receive the support they need - no matter how traumatized they may be - when estranged from their families. So rascal monks and trickster gurus find ways to attract their money.

It is impossible to standardize the abstract paradigm of spirituality, so new age practitioners and teachers are not accountable to any quality control system. The domain of spiritual, psychic and alternative consulting is a blessing for new age tricksters.

There are myriad routes from the material world of separation and conflict to the divine realm of unity and harmony. There is no right or wrong way. However many spiritual masters warn their disciples against delving into other spiritual practices, either because *"their way is the only legitimate way"* or because they demand exclusive commitment by their followers. If such gurus don't need the money or the popularity, why do so many try so hard to retain their followers?

There is no evidence that Gypsy Rose Lee's channeled information really originated from Archangel Michael or Kwan Yin; perhaps the messages are from demonic entities? There are other possibilities – maybe the gypsy has a penchant for creative storytelling or she projects her own psychological issues onto her vulnerable clients.

The key paradox resides in the basis of spirituality - unconditional love. Any spiritual teacher who charges a fee for his wisdom is offering conditional love, thereby applying a third dimensional reward structure to a fifth dimensional service. Some healers and so-called spiritual masters charge upwards of $1,000 per consultation – hardly unconditional love.

Terry the Tarot, author of several books about tarot, is an example of an adept psychic trickster. Terry originally trained with the commercial cult known as Scientology.[25] Afterwards he established a tarot training centre in north London. He held regular open evenings to allow his graduates to practice their psychic abilities on the lay public. Terry, like many new age *"masters"*, slept with many of his voluptuous female students. He instructed his trainees to give their clients *"any old flannel"* during readings. And at a party of psychics he took the hostess' camera with him to the toilet to capture an image of his member for her.

Bhagwan Rajneesh, later known as Osho, was the veritable mystic trickster guru from Poona, India, who preached what his aspirants wanted to hear. He gained massive popularity with disenchanted middle class f**kups by advocating free sex as a natural extension of Tantric Buddhism. Osho is reputed to have collected 93 Rolls Royce cars with the money donated by his followers.

Osho claimed he experienced enlightenment at the age of twenty-one.[26] He was highly charismatic, a vital characteristic of every cult leader; and his techniques were radical. Osho introduced social meditations[27] requiring his aspirants to undergo primal catharsis to the sound of music.

Osho legitimized madness[28] in his following quote:

"Watch a madman, because a madman has fallen out of society. Society means the fixed world of roles, games. A madman is mad because he has no fixed role now, he has fallen out: he is the perfect dropout. A sage is also a perfect dropout in a different dimension. He is not mad; in fact he is the only possibility of pure sanity. But the whole world is mad, fixed – that's why a sage looks mad. Watch a madman: that is the look which is needed."

The stresses and strains of modern living support a burgeoning demand for commercial psychotherapy cults; and Avatar is one such example. Harry Palmer, previously extricated from the Church of Scientology cult, is Avatar's charismatic founder.

Palmer lifted many of Scientology's techniques and reinvented himself as a paternal visionary and proponent of an *"enlightened planetary civilization"*.[35] Palmer misrepresented his credentials by claiming he had an MA in educational psychology (when he actually studied English). So although he has no credentials in psychology, he assures his ardent disciples he reads lots of books.

Avatar is an educational multi-level marketing (MLM) cult. This means that Palmer established a pyramid-like commercial structure to reward his loyal disciples. Business introducers receive a percentage of their recruits' workshop fees and many Avatar *"masters"* make a living by spreading the word of Palmer's vision of an enlightened planetary civilization.

Avatar workshops are promoted as meeting the delegate's needs. The workshops get progressively more expensive; and immense sales effort is invested by Avatar *"masters"* to sign up customers for the subsequent course. The goal of every Avatar devotee is attendance of the Avatar *Wizards* course. Everyone on the Wizards course is seemingly happy for its duration of thirteen days. The cost of the *Wizards* course is $10,000 (exclusive of travel, accommodation and expenses). Enough said.

Throughout Asia, stories abound of trickster monks who use orange robes as a means of disguise to extort money from gullible wannabe do-gooders. Sometimes newspapers report rascal monks fornicating with their girlfriends and even peddling amphetamines.

In Thailand, many Buddhist novice monks wear robes as a means of bringing merit and social repute to their family; but not necessarily to improve themselves. The orange robe is merely a symbol of spiritual elevation and social responsibility; what occurs underneath is another matter.

One female shaman interviewed described herself as a *"spiritual Mafioso"*. Her primary business was deforestation and arbitrage - importing teak from Myanmar and paying off government officials.

Energy practitioners apply the natural laws of the universe for the benefit of mankind ... or to its detriment. There are plenty of competent spiritual consultants and shamans out there, but how many apply their skills compassionately and with unconditional love? Sadly too many shamans are goaded into using black magic on behalf of their clients who relish revenge upon their adversaries. Whether magic is black and white depends upon the intention.

Spiritual consultancy or shamanism is the perfect career for the trickster. There are no professional standards; and training credentials are irrelevant. There is no accountability; and negligence never results in punitive damages. Furthermore their vulnerable clients elevate them as gurus or masters, hanging onto every word they utter. And since there are no ethical rules, they can fornicate with as many of their devotees as they please.

Charismatic tricksters sometimes start up their own cults. There are four main types of cult: religious, political, psychotherapy / educational and commercial cults.[30] Most cults promise to rectify their followers' emotional damage with their magic formula. Instead cults brainwash their subjects with their dogma, and destroy their independence and self-esteem.

Jesus as Trickster

Christ is described as a trickster in the South American Quechua lore which is associated with tribal shamanism. One tale from twentieth century Imbabura tells of the infant Christ transforming two bullies into pigs. This story resembles trickster tales from the *"Infancy gospels of the New testament Apocrypha"*.[31]

Quechua lore states that Jesus evaded Roman soldiers by transforming himself into a silk-cotton tree when they tried to capture him in Bethlehem. On another occasion Christ turned into a rooster to avoid being seized by the authorities.

One South American folklore story cites Christ asking a farmer what he was doing as he planted wheat. Christ's question annoyed the farmer who subsequently replied sarcastically, *"I'm planting stones!"* Jesus said *"So be it,"* and the following day the field was full of stones. This dark tale is the antithesis of the New Testament's *"Parable of the Sower"*[37] which uses stones as a metaphor for ignorance (or obstacles to faith in God).

There is plenty of evidence to support the hypothesis that Jesus was a rebel who held radical views. For example, the New Testament[36] describes Jesus angrily overturning the tables of the money-changers at the temple and accusing them of turning it into *"a den of thieves"*. If he were alive today, surely he would be a critic of the World Trade Organization (WTO).

The rascal guru Bhagwan Rajneesh (Osho) reported evidence that the trickster Christ never died on the cross.[32]

In a conspiracy between a rich sympathizer and Pontius Pilate, Jesus was removed from the cross after only six hours of crucifixion. Although Jesus was unconscious, he was not dead when he was taken away to a cave. Jesus' followers transported him from Judea to Kashmir, India, where he recuperated and lived until the age of 112.

Trickster Bhagwan Rajneesh claimed he visited the graves of Jesus and Moses in Kashmir. The writing on their grave stones is in Hebrew and neither grave pointed towards Mecca unlike Muslim graves. Jesus' gravestone bears the name *"Joshua"* which is the Hebrew translation of Jesus (the Christian version). A Jewish family has been looking after both graves in a village called Pahalgam for centuries.

Of course there is massive evidence that Jesus was a wise rebel. If Jesus was alive today he would surely be branded an anarchist, and perhaps destined to spend time in a penitentiary or mental asylum... unless his trickster cunning and wit would enable him to evade his adversaries.

To conclude, Jesus possessed the magical healing abilities of a shaman; the non-conformist attitude of a punk; and the trickster characteristics of both punks and shamans.

The Punk Monk and the Drunk

The following trickster tale is based upon the Chinese folktale *"The Monk and the Drunk"* which dates back to the Ming dynasty (1368-1644).[38]

There once lived a sly monk whose inclination, whenever he brushed against the law, was to sKurt around it, duck and dive underneath it, bend or twist it, and ultimately break it. He was known as Slimy, because somehow, he always managed to slip off the scales of justice.

One day, however, he was caught stealing and sent under guard to the capital for trial. With one end of the rope around his neck and the other end in the guard's fist, it seemed that even Slimy wouldn't be able to slip out of the law's stranglehold this time. But there were still several days to go before they would reach the capital; so the guard and his captive had to stay at an inn along the way.

When they settled down for dinner and the rope around the monk's neck loosened, to enable him to swallow his food, the innkeeper brought several bottles of wine to the table, for Slimy had secretly ordered them during the flurry of their arrival.

"Let's drink a toast to our journey together," said the crafty monk, jovially. *"You are an exceptionally good guard, and now I know my game is over. I admire your abilities so much. Certainly you will be praised by the Emperor himself, but, alas, it will be too late for me to express my admiration personally, for I shall be languishing in prison by then, following your commendable actions. So let's drink to your success, and may you live forever with honors heaped upon you!"*

The guard, flattered by the compliments of the infamous monk, drank the wine with gusto. He proceeded to empty the several bottles of wine, with the encouragement of Slimy, until he was a stupefied drunk lying senselessly on the floor.

The cunning monk did not waste a moment. He shaved off the guard's hair, and took the rope from his neck and placed it around the drunken guard's head. Then the wily monk disappeared into the shadows of the night.

When the guard woke up the following morning, he staggered around the inn looking for his prisoner. When he scratched his fuzzy head, he was shocked to discover that he had no hair. Then he became aware of the rope around his neck. Aghast, his mouth fell open and he fell to the ground in a crumpled heap, exclaiming,

"If I am the monk, where is my guard?"

Tricksters R Us

Earth is a beautiful planet with plenty of rich and varied resources to go around its residents. Most of the planet's inhabitants simply want a stable and secure existence without conflict. But unfortunately the human race – the trickster's trickster - deceived itself by subscribing to *The Lie* which caused untold misery for the majority.

The Lie encompasses the myth of scarcity, notions of good and evil, the need for competition and compliance to survive, the belief that solutions to our problems can be purchased externally, and the supremacy of quantity over quality of life. *The Lie* is leached into the collective unconscious of the globe's lemming-led brothers and sisters; it dictates that if we try hard – ever so obediently – we will receive rewards commensurate with our efforts – this may be true, as long as we tell ourselves a few 'porky pies' along the way.[41]

"Working for a rise [to] better my station
[to] take my baby to sophistication
[I've] seen the ads; she thinks it's nice
Better work hard - I've seen the price
Clocks go slow in a place of work
Minutes drag and the hours jerk
You're frettin', you're sweatin'
But did you notice you're not getting anywhere?"
- The Clash[42]

So what would it feel like 'getting somewhere'? Perhaps feeling accepted unconditionally? Why should it be necessary to *"prove oneself"* or achieve some arbitrary goal to *"be somebody"*. Such is the outcome of society based upon competition. It's supposedly not enough just to *"let it be,"* and be oneself.

Here are the lies that we, as tricksters, subscribe to:

The Myth of Scarcity dictates that consumable products are in short supply, so we must compete fiercely for them. We do so by working like dogs according to an elaborate framework of *"civilized"* rules which cause economic concentration in specific areas of power; and the adept players make it seem effortless on TV.

Moralist Masochism, underpinned by concepts of good and evil, is upheld by priests and other authorities to control the laity. William Blake defined *"good"* as *"the passive that obeys reason"*; and *"evil"* as *"the active springing from energy.* [43] *"* Our societal system, therefore, pressures us to repress *"evil"* in our personal unconscious...where it will lurk in the darkest recesses of the underworld, awaiting a chance to escape...

*"Ah, they're messing with the forces of Good and Evil
They turn 'em loose, they turn into people"*
- David Byrne[45]

Our global **Total Quantity Management** (TQM) system states that progress can be measured in economic terms. So, according to TQM, everyone can contribute to the evolutionary development of planet Earth by consuming more and working harder to purchase more stuff. Numbers rule, but the cost is sacrificed quality of life, wellbeing and unity.

The trickster's trickster is **Outward Looking for Solutions** (OLS) to their problems. The prevailing belief is that our problems will disappear if we pay an expert for a course of consultations. The reality is that only our soul has the intelligence to liberate us from the manacles of disease… so we should seek solutions by looking inwards – not the other way around.

The Myth of Immortality dictates that life is so precious that we must lengthen it at all costs – to the detriment of life quality. Fear of death (and enlightenment) prevents most people from really living life to the full. This myth impedes risk-taking and pursuit of passion.

The Parents know Best fallacy causes untold misery. Children are born geniuses, tampered with by ignoramuses, and die as blithering idiots. Religions attribute godlike custodianship to parents over their infant chattels, so parents are always deemed right, and kids, always wrong.

Free Market Economics guarantees instability, where *"boom and bust"* cycles are like night and day…yet most

81

people want a secure and stable life. The big money is made by financial speculators while those who really contribute to the planet's wellbeing – the farmers and laborers – try to get by. The trickster's system reacts to greed (boom) and fear (doom – or bust).

CHAPTER 3

HOW OUTSIDERS LOVE ASIA

Outsider Art

The word Outsider which was introduced at the beginning of the nineteenth century is defined as:

1. a person who does not belong to a particular group
2. chiefly British: a contender not expected to win[1]

Society's outsider is detached from his or her family and community, and usually vilified for being different from the rest.

Synonyms for Outsider include floater, intruder, odd one out and refugee[2]. Since the outsider has no home, love or support, he or she has ultimate freedom to be anyone they please to be. Therefore there are strong links between outsiderdom, vagrancy and itinerancy.

Authentic punks are outsiders who have an urgent need to express their truth via their chosen art-form. Whereas shamans are summoned by their host spirits and subjected to paranormal experiences – commonly perceived in *"developed society"* as mental illness - outsider artists are summoned by their souls to express their truth, usually following dire and traumatic circumstances which turn their world upside down.

George Orwell wrote the slogan, *"The price of freedom is insecurity.*[3] *"* The price tag to which Orwell refers covers myriad painful emotions from loneliness and anxiety to anger and depression; often physical hardship without any economic cushion or social support; and vilification and blame for being different or outside - surely the salt that is rubbed deep within their wounds.

The trump card of every f**k-up is potential for freedom and innovative art. The greatest art is created by outsiders who risk everything, while insiders concentrate on making money within the comfort and beauty of established mainstream systems.

"If you're going to subvert and do something that's truly great, you can't do it from the inside ... If you don't just do it with the money in mind then you can stay on the outside and concentrate on being great. As soon as your money becomes a serious concern for you, you're compromised."
- Johnny Marr[4]

The spirit of Godlike genius refuses to be compromised by mundane concerns, especially money. Of course everyone needs money to survive, but whenever money is the primary focus, the magical essence of the genie disappears. Therefore outsider artists achieve mastery by focusing upon perfection of their art unless lack of money limits their pursuits.

Black Sheep

The Black Sheep is an idiom used to describe an outsider, a disgrace, an embarrassment, ne'er-do-well or disreputable member of a group, especially within a family.

Occasionally black sheep were born into herds of white sheep. Farmers considered black sheep undesirable because their wool could not be dyed and therefore they commanded a lower economic market value.

In Greek mythology black sheep were sacrificed in honor of Hades, God of the Underworld.[8] Also the French term *bete noire*, which literally means 'black beast', applies to something either disliked or feared.

The Party God, Dionysus is the God of exiles, outsider black sheep and aliens. Dionysus, also known as Bacchus and *"The Liberator"*, is the God of *"foreign origins"*. The Liberator, son of Zeus, uses punk music and wine to transform stress and worry into pure uplifting energy.

Black sheep are outcasts. In the Indian caste system, disgraced members of a social stratum are thrown out of their community. Amidst India's societal dregs at the bottom of the barrel lie 'the untouchables'.

"In psychology, a black sheep is the member of a rigidly triangulated family who holds the rest tightly together by being identified as the bad, sick or deviant one who causes all the family problems. In this situation the rule enforcer in the family is charged with the job of controlling the black sheep from revealing the family secrets. The black sheep is seen as the outsider, but only because he is the teller of truth.[5]"

Joe Strummer was influenced by American folk songwriter Tim Hardin who wrote the song, *Black Sheep Boy*. Hardin, who served Uncle Sam in the Vietnam War, died of a heroin and morphine overdose in 1980.[42]

The Vietnam War created many psychologically damaged outsiders amongst its veterans other than Tim Hardin.

Alan Parker's movie, *Birdy*, is about two men who served in the war and who subsequently struggled to fit back into civilian life. One of the men, Birdy, went over the edge with his obsession about birds and even endeavored to act out his fantasy of flying like a bird. The music for *Birdy* was written by Peter Gabriel.[49]

Julian Cope published the *Black Sheep Album*, the result of his exploration of what it is to be an outsider in modern western culture.[6] Cope colorfully emblazoned Carl Jung's following quotation across his album cover: *"Resistance to the organized mass can be effected only by the man who is as well organized as the mass itself."*

Cope illuminates the concept of Outsider Art by *"social outcasts who use their obstinacy and strength of personality to carve a path for themselves in the normal world."*[7]

Cope also reminds us that the most famous black sheep and punk monk is the prophet Jesus Christ who was rejected by his own people. Christ was known for speaking the truth and being a bugbear to his presiding authorities. As George Bernard Shaw said, *"If you're going to tell the truth, make them laugh otherwise they'll kill you."* Perhaps Christ just needed to hone his skills as a standup comedian.

Thankfully Jesus Christ brought hope to black sheep outsiders with his *Parable of the Prodigal Son*. Christ effectively rubber-stamped timeout for reckless living – sex and drugs and rock and roll – but for God's sake, make lifestyle amends before your demise, otherwise there'll be no fattened calf - perhaps just a vegetarian spring roll suitable for the likes of Saint Morrissey, author of *Meat is Murder.*[28]

Rank Outsider

The rank outsider is believed to have little chance of winning. Indeed outsiders – including mavericks, misfits, eccentrics and freaks – are commonly dubbed losers simply because they are different and don't fit in (to another person's game plan).

Punk is a haven for many rank outsiders unable to establish roots elsewhere. Insiders impose their rigid and elitist formulas to maintain their comfortable and complacent state of separation. So insiders use credit status and acquisitions as a measure of success, but these things are meaningless to tortured souls.

"It is through art, and through art only, that we can realize our perfection; through art and art only, that we can shield ourselves from the sordid perils of actual existence"
- Oscar Wilde

Oscar Wilde's life was a work of art, which is evidence that he was doomed from the beginning. *"He was both enthusiastically perverse and a keen invert, which means he gleefully turned conventional wisdom upside down and knavishly assaulted traditional attitudes, something any star worth its twinkle would want to do."*[19]

The outsider survives by thinking differently from the insider, desperately seeking ways to express himself and not caring what others think of him; a tall challenge, since most outsiders are extra-sensory perceivers. Perhaps God played a cruel trick by giving thicker skins to insiders – the ones who don't need them.

87

The insider immerses himself in a competition where success is easily quantifiable; but numbers are meaningless to the purveyor of truth … for he cares only about the authenticity of his message and the quality of his being. If insiders and outsiders are competing in different races, then who is the real winner – the inside empire builder in the race to be richest, or the outsider artist, champion of his own human race?

"I do a job I really, really love and I have fun with. People think you can't be grown up unless you're moaning about your job"
- Robert Smith, The Cure[20]

Godlike genius Robert Smith[30] asserts that people who pursue their own passionate desires – rather than ego-driven craving for recognition – are real winners, even if they never achieve success, because at least they experienced what they enjoy most. The outsider who actively pursues passion cannot really lose when his heart and soul is singing joyfully.

Where is Outsiderdom?

Ostracism was considered the ultimate form of social castration in Great Britain. *"To send a person to Coventry"* is a British idiom which means ostracism of an outsider.
The idiom, *"to send to Coventry"* means *"to ostracize somebody and arose from the inhabitants of Coventry's distaste for soldiers, to the extent that any woman seen speaking to one was immediately ostracized; consequently any soldier sent to Coventry was also ostracized by its townsfolk."*[15]

Is Coventry really such a bad place?

"I can think of worse places to be
Like down in the streets or in the sewer
Or even on the end of a skewer!"
- The Stranglers[16]

Anyway, where do outsiders choose to live in exile after being rejected by their family or community?

Nick Leeson, the rogue commodity trader who instigated the downfall of Barings Bank in 1995, chose Ireland. Leeson exceeded Thatcher's *"Greed is Good"* byline with his impressive GBP 3.7 billion fraud which earned him over four years in prison (following time in Coventry). Afterwards – as a reward for his bad behaviour - Leeson was appointed Chief Executive of Galway Football Club.[17]

Ronnie Biggs, the bank robber and musical associate of the Sex Pistols chose exile in the warmer climes of Brazil during his 36 year sabbatical from prison. Biggs was a partner in the gang which carried out the *Great Train Robbery* in 1963 before venturing into punk rock in the party city of Rio de Janeiro.[37]

Punk monk and spiritual escape artist Dr Tuesday Lobsang Rampa, who claimed to be a lama in Tibet before incarnating into the body of an English plumber, immigrated to Canada after doing time in Coventry (followed by a stint in Ireland). The British media lambasted Rampa venomously, branding him a fake. Meanwhile another outsider called David Mellor - Joe Strummer's brother - was an ardent reader of Rampa's quasi-mystical books shortly before his suicide.

89

"Whatever David's thoughts on Rampa's authenticity, the books offered a mysterious and exciting world, an escape."[18]

Legends John Lydon and John Lennon chose to base themselves in California and New York respectively. And according to the mystic trickster, Osho, Jesus Christ chose Kashmir.

Confusion

Colin Wilson, author of The Outsider, noted that the outsider's world is irrational and chaotic; whereas the establishment figure inhabits the rational world of order.

*"When [the outsider] asserts his sense of anarchy in the face of the bourgeois' complacent acceptance, it is not simply the need to cock a snook at respectability that provokes him; it is the distressing sense that **truth must be told at all costs**, otherwise there can be no hope for an ultimate restoration of order. Even if there seems no room for hope, truth must be told... The Outsider is a man who has awakened to chaos."*[9]

At some point in the outsider's life, his (or her) picture of reality was shattered, causing an urgent quest for meaning amid the resulting carnage. Perhaps he relied upon belief systems which later collapsed like dominos when put to the test. Afterwards, without any valid support system, the outsider discovers an alternative reality: confusion.

"You just can't believe me when I show you what you mean to me;
You just can't believe me when I show you what you cannot see;

You're hiding from feelings, searching for more
Sharing and hoping, untouched for so long"
- New Order, from the song, *Confusion*[10]

According to the insider, the outsider failed society and therefore he should be disgraced and ideally vilified. The outsider's crime was falling through a black hole - somewhere in the system - and not being sufficiently insensitive to deny the ensuing pain. Insiders obey the maxim, *Boys don't Cry*, but such denial is not a viable option for the outsider.[11]

Wilson's Outsider *"is not sure who he is. He has found an "I", but it is not the true "I". His main business is to find his way back to himself.*[12] *"* And this is not an easy task for the lone fall guy floating atrophically in space. Another Wilson – Tony Wilson of Manchester – was portrayed in the documentary *24 Hour Party People* as not knowing who he really was.[23]

"Feeling easy on the outside
But not so funny on the inside"
- Blue Oyster Cult[46]

In the novel, *Walk on the Wild Side*, Nelson Algren questioned why *"lost people develop into greater human beings than those who have never been lost in their whole lives."* Lou Reed was influenced by Algren's novel and wrote a song about underworld life under the same title.[13]

The punk metaphysical model - explained later - helps to show why it's necessary to be lost and confused before achieving Godlike genius. This *"healing crisis"* is called the Transition; and it represents the disintegration of old ways (aligned with disease) and the simultaneous development of new ways (supporting wellbeing). There are no shortcuts, so every Godlike genius must pass through the turbulence of the transition which manifests itself in feelings of confusion.

How does it Feel?

How does it feel to be an outsider?

The outsider has something missing from his life – love. He is typically burdened by sinking feelings of emptiness, loneliness and deep fears about never being good enough. The outsider's urgent quest, therefore, is to make sense of his f**ked up world. But what comes first – a loving relationship partner, a place to call home, or a stable means to a living? How can he attract love into his life?

Let's capture the essence of the outsider for a moment. His stride lacks confidence; doubts surface as he approaches each crossroad. When he looks at women they respond angrily with a grimace as they look away. He knows that anything beautiful belongs to others.

"Shakes in the chemists while buying his vits
Puts his head down when girls pass in the street"
- The Fall[22]

The outsider is the detached and isolated observer whose real currency is insight; but currency must be tradable, otherwise it's worthless. Therefore the outsider urgently needs a medium through which he can express his insights; otherwise his mind will stagnate and poison him ultimately.

Every outsider dreams about a secret hideaway to call home. Outsider Joe Strummer said he used to fantasize about living under the metal structures which support advertising billboards. Instead Strummer lived in a squat in London while he played with the band, The 101ers.[47]

The outsider's plight is so simple and yet so complex: nothing works; nothing fits and nobody understands. The dreamer may grasp onto a transient goal, panacea or formulaic solution for an instant... until inevitable disillusionment shatters the cognitive mosaic into a trillion fractals... and he submerges again into the toxic effluents of his mind.

"By 2001, also sprach Zarathustra
It pays to talk to on-one...
This is the Spring without end
This is the Summer of malcontent
This is the Winter of your mind"
- The Fall[24]

Of course not all outsiders feel the same way as the *"Smiths Trinity"* (Mark E. Smith, Robert Smith (The Cure) and The Smiths). Enlightened outsiders such as Jesus Christ and John Lennon felt differently, which is why they were considered an impending threat to the establishment. The authorities crucified Christ for expressing his unique version of the truth; and John Lennon was assassinated, providing fertile fodder for conspiracy theorists... Every outsider has a cross to bear...

Outsiderdom begins at Home

Research evidence suggests that outsiders who express themselves falsely were cajoled into their situation by controlling parents, unable to love their children uncondition-ally. Adolescents construct a *"false self"* while pretending to be the kind of person whom his parents will love; while others react rebelliously against their parents' controlling behavior.[14]

"A crack on the head is what you get for not asking; and a crack on the head is what you get for asking"
- The Smiths[19]

Children who are encouraged to express themselves naturally, and who are neither punished for *"bad be-havior"* nor rewarded for *"good behavior"* – especially during their first seven years of development – become happier and more confident than their heavily criticized colleagues.

Many children suffer physical violence and poverty in under-privileged families. Some kids run away from their abusive parental home to a life of institutionalization while others find support somewhere in the punk subculture.

"I'd like to drop my trousers to the Queen
Every sensible child will know what this means
The poor and the needy, the sick and the greedy, on her
terms and if the day came when I felt a natural emotion
I'd get such a shock I'd probably jump in the ocean"
- The Smiths[39]

Abuse in over-privileged families tends to be emo-tional rather than physical in nature by calculating class-conscious bigots. Children of these toxic parents have no physical scars to show social workers because their dam-age is invisible; and they are not so welcome inside the

punk movement (unlike their delinquent proletariat coun-
terparts) due to the thorn in their backside of their inher-
ited class orientation. So, with nowhere to go for support,
the likes of *"privileged"* David Mellor (Joe Strummer's
brother) committed suicide. Joe Strummer survived by
played the trickster's card like John Peel, downwardly re-
vising his *"privileged"* social background to gain acceptance of the punk movement.

*"We're going to have to learn to live together and de-
velop a greater tolerance and get rid of whatever our fa-
thers gave us in the way of hatred between nations"*
- Joe Strummer, 2000[40]

Radio deejay John Peel was a *"privileged"* outsider
from an emotionally constipated (unloving) conservative
family. Peel was raped by another pupil inside a public
convenience during his time at boarding school in Shrewsbury. The deejay never discussed his childhood sexual or-
deal until three years before he died.[44] Privileged boys are
constantly reminded how lucky they are … and any boy
telling *"secrets"* – or *"sneaking"* - is ruthlessly punished
by the establishment.

"We don't need no education
We don't need no thought control
No dark sarcasm in the classroom
Teacher, leave those kids alone!"
- Pink Floyd[45]

Karl Marx coined the phrase, *"blessed is he that hath
no family."* The orphan's coin reveals rootlessness on one
side and liberation on the other. Psychologist Dr. Susan
Forward asserted that *"toxic parents"* damage their chil-

dren by abusing them and treating them as chattels under their Godlike custodianship. *"What better word than Toxic to describe parents who inflict ongoing trauma, abuse and denigration on their children?"*[29]

"Baby lying in a womb
Are you free or in a tomb?"
- Budgie[43]

Jim Morrison, singer of The Doors, was estranged from his authoritarian middle class family. Young Morrison was frequently *"dressed down"* military style, which means berating the child until he was reduced to tears and acknowledged his failings. After graduation at UCLA, Morrison broke off contact with his family and later claimed his family was dead.[36]

Options for Outsiders

How the outsider can save himself depends upon his wellbeing, economic status and his values.

Conventional wisdom dictates that the outsider's panacea lies somewhere outside: in religion, new age therapies, self-help books, drugs and institutions. This process, *"Outside Inwards"*, is a boon for the global economy since the outsider pays his money to be fixed. Consumer solutions tend to offer mere glimpses of hope and transient gratification – like the pharmaceutical and self-help industries – designed for lives of addiction and loyal repeat business.

Just imagine Governments coming clean and broadcasting, *"We understand that your parents f**ked you up.*

Just get used to it. Nothing short of death with fix your damage. Drugs don't work. Therapy may offer temporary respite, but it's akin to sticking plasters on a fractured arm."

The alternative journey to recovery necessitates a personal journey of spiritual excavation – or soul mining[21] - and creative expression as *"insider art"* (such as punk music) or a shamanic journey to the underworld to bring aspects of our subconscious to the surface.

"I think people have got to find where their direction lies and channel their violence into music or something creative"
- Mick Jones[35]

However extraordinary spiritual outsiders are special exceptions to the above rule. The spiritual outsider of *"developed nations"* would likely be a respected insider in tribal communities. Strange boys who experience paranormal visions – evidence of involuntary shamanic initiation - are prime targets for school bullies in modern civilization, so without special support, these children are destined for introversion, a life on medication or even mental institutionalization.

The mystic psychologist Carl G. Jung had childhood paranormal experiences indicative of a shaman. Jung studied psychiatry and hobnobbed with the likes of sex-fixated Sigmund Freud; so he was able to explore his complex mind within la crème de la crème of academia and his own psychiatry practice.

Walk-ins are highly evolved people who involuntarily host a new spirit after losing their previous spirit. The change of spirit typically causes intense trauma – manifesting emotional instability and a plethora of disease symptoms – rendering the walk-in unable to live a normal life until their physical body harmonizes energetically with their new spirit (which may never happen).

Perhaps walk-ins would become shamans inside indigenous tribes; but the options are less enticing in modern developed society unless a cushion of wealth is available to them. These traumatized patients may be treated by suitable healers, such as lightbody integration practitioners.[25] However those less fortunate, who lack appropriate support, are destined for a life of medical institutionalization or other pseudo-suicide.

"I only wish that I could see yesterday
The same way as I can see tomorrow"
- Alex Harvey[38]

Damaged souls were screwed up during their childhood by abusive parents, standardized *"one size fits all"* education systems and other authority figures. The omnipotent doctrine of competition, which dominates the education system, creates and separates winners and losers. The kids are graded and degraded.

Outsider Art

Creative self-expression is probably the healthiest option for any outsider, but not all outsiders have the necessary mettle for the arduous journey to the zenith of self-realization. The key prerequisite is faith – stubborn relentless blind faith in self and the cosmos.

The outsider must protect himself against the ravages of life, especially rampant caustic criticism and disillusionment during emotional recessions and economic depressions. Sometimes the journey may seem like a series of horrendous blind dates; Chrissie Hynde and Deborah Harry show up only in the wettest and wildest of dreams.

Author George Orwell, born as Eric Blair, was one of history's most misunderstood outsiders. Orwell began his career with the Imperial Police in Myanmar in January 1924 instead of studying at university.[26] In Mandalay Orwell developed a reputation for not fitting in. He was described by his colleague as *"sallow-faced, tall, thin, and gangling, whose clothes, no matter how well cut, seemed to hang on him."*[27] He was socially inept, preferring to read alone voraciously.

Orwell developed a keen sense of the British class system during his school years. He was always perceived as the poor boy in a class of rich kids from prestigious families; and his alienation was compounded by perpetual ill-health, especially respiratory problems, which prevented him from excelling in sports. So Orwell developed into a social misfit with interests in nature, politics and black magic.[32]

Perhaps Orwell's social humiliation was shared by Joe Strummer and his brother, David. Strummer's father *"held a fairly lowly position"* in the diplomatic service, so Strummer was judged as *"relatively humble stock"* by his boarding school compatriots.[41]

Orwell was irrevocably affected by the brutality he witnessed during his duty in Burma as an Imperial Police officer. These haunting images tipped Orwell into the alternative reality of derelicts, paupers, prostitutes and drug addicts.[34]

"Personally I would not speak so lightly of murder. It so happens that I have seen the bodies of numbers of murdered men – I don't mean killed in battle, I mean murdered... Therefore I have some conception of what murder means – the terror, the hatred, the howling relatives, the post-mortems, the blood, the smells."
- George Orwell[33]

Orwell's life story is that of a social underling, being pushed by obsequious class-conscious parents into social paradigms *"out of reach"*. Since Orwell felt like an outsider to privileged society, he sympathized with victims of imperialist oppression. Orwell's sensitivity to oppression spurred him to write about Big Brother in his satire, *Nineteen Eighty Four*.

Kurt Cobain was another great outsider artist who shot to fame, struggled with drug addiction and fell over the edge. When asked what he thought of Cobain's suicide, Morrissey replied caustically, *"I respect his decision."*[31]

Godlike outsider artists exist in every realm of art. Outsider writers include *Noam Chomsky, Jon Pilger, George Monbiot, William Blake, Oscar Wilde, Aldous Huxley* and *Robert Fisk*. The list of outsider musicians includes *Jim Morrison, Ian Curtis, John Lydon* and *Amadeus Mozart*.

Plight of Outsiders

History contains countless cases of outsider-innovators being fleeced by insider-strategic managers.

"God only acts and is, in existing beings or men. These two classes of men are always upon Earth, and they should be enemies; whoever tries to reconcile them seeks to destroy existence"
- William Blake[48]

A battle between insiders and outsiders occurred in 1940 after Jerry Siegel and Joe Shuster introduced *Superman* to the world. An identical concept had been launched by the genius outsider Philip G. Wylie one decade earlier under *"The Gladiator"* title. So Wylie sued the creators of superman for blatant plagiarism - and won.

Wylie's *Gladiator* was transformed into a movie in 1978 by Richard Donner. Wylie's hero, who possessed superhuman gifts, was unable to find his place in the world. In the movie's climax, the hero is struck by lightning while asking questions about God, apparently reflecting the author's religious doubts.

Revised Definitions

Clearly revision of our existing definitions of *Outsider* and *Insider* is overdue. Alternative definitions follow:

An Outsider is a person who risks everything to save his soul, by expressing his unique version of truth. The outsider necessarily experiences chaos as a stepping stone en route to Godlike genius.

101

An Insider is a person who risks nothing - other than subjugation of his soul - while striving for profit and status by conforming to the dictates and illusions of the consensus. The Insider is the manipulative *"adaptor"* and agent of heartless plagiarism who lives an orderly extra-ordinary life, devoid of passion.

How Outsiders Love Asia

A Bangkok expat commented that Thailand's expat community comprises outsiders, losers and criminals.

Northern Thailand – notably, Chiang Mai – has seemingly developed into an international rehab centre. Damaged foreigners from around the globe rush to Chiang Mai for healing, meditation and yoga, fasting and detox treatments, while alcoholics and addicts head for Twelve Steps groups - Alcoholics Anonymous (AA), Narcotics Anonymous (NA), Codependents Anonymous (Coda) or Meditators Anonymous (MA).

The above-mentioned Twelve Steps groups are suited for addicts, or people who need some external stimulation to fill the void within. Several members of these Twelve Steps groups admitted to simply substituting drug addiction with sex addiction... yet another potentially abusive pastime.

CHAPTER 4

GLOBALIZATION OF MALCONTENT

Global Transition

Despite growing affluence and amazing technological achievements, people in the US and Europe are no happier than people were during the 1950s according to *The Economist*. The New Economics Foundation reports that quality of life has actually fallen in the UK since 1976. British people are wealthier than ever, but less happy.

Many people feel their quality of life eroding as they need to work longer hours to maintain their standard of living. Side effects of our money-driven life include stress and depression, drug addiction, crime epidemics and family breakdown.

There are more opportunities than ever for winners able to manage the pace of change. However there are a growing number of losers in the stampede for money and power.

Our planet is in transition between the old fear-based paradigm and the new way of happiness. Global instability will continue until we adopt a new vision based upon real world progress.

Economic Progress

Currently progress is measured using Gross Domestic Product (GDP).

GDP is the annual total market value of a country's production of goods and services. Therefore economic activity – buying and selling of consumer products – increases our index of progress.

Since World War II, GDP has been adopted by world leaders as the main indicator of progress.

Political leaders are responsible for making policies which maximise the country's adopted index of progress. They have been successful in their task of boosting GDP.

There are many ways of boosting economic activity other than buying and selling consumer goods. Crime, disease, family breakdown and war also increase GDP.

Theft stimulates the economy via the replacement of stolen and damaged goods; it also enhances public perception of the need for insurance, burglar alarms and surveillance technology.

Family breakdown is a boon for the economy. Usually the family unit splits into two separate economies; this means the running of two households instead of one. Lawyers charge fees for their work in divorce proceedings; Removals companies move personal effects to the second home. Now there are two periodic gas bills, two telephone bills and two electricity bills, whereas there was only one of each before.

One aspect of uncontrolled economic growth is environmental pollution. Many factories discharge toxic waste into rivers. Some of this damage may be irreversible. However, if the government decides to clean up the pollution, effectively subsidising the factory, this cost is actually added to GDP figure. Therefore pollution enhances economic progress. The irreversible damage caused by the factory is not accounted for whatsoever.

Similarly, wars inflate GDP with the cost of bombing and the cost of reconstruction. Each US$100 billion spent on bombs used probably creates in excess of US$1000 billion worth of reconstruction contracts. Every person injured in war required medical treatment so pharmaceutical companies benefit from war.

The world has changed in many ways since the introduction of GDP. Notably, barriers to free trade have been removed. Financial markets are easily destabilised by speculators. The world is not safe while GDP is used to measure progress without solid social, moral and ethical foundations to offer real stability.

GDP is like a household Quality of Life indicator. The household progress is measured according to its consumption. However, of the five householders, only one person has money to buy anything. The single buyer does not share the products with the other four householders. The economically inactive householders simply watch the gluttony of the single consumer.

Many economists have conceded that increased GDP does not necessarily improve quality of life. Now many organisations and nations are developing their own quality of life indicators to measure real progress. Bhutan, which lies between India and China, uses *"Gross Domestic Happiness"* (GDH) as their country's main quality of life indicator. In Atlanta, Canada, a Genuine Progress Index

(GPI) is being developed. New Zealand has created its own quality of life index.

The seeds of change are being planted now.

Real Progress

Real progress is a world population which is getting happier.

Happiness is the goal of the new quality-oriented development model. Money is used only as the means to achieving happiness; it is not the goal - unlike GDP.

The evolutionary journey to happiness, and ultimately enlightenment, is congruent with Buddhist philosophy. Enlightenment is the highest state of consciousness possible on planet Earth; it is characterised by feelings of unconditional love, compassion, joy and unity. Buddhists are known for their cheerful and peaceful disposition.

Happiness is aligned with sustainability, efficiency and unity. Energy is used more efficiently with cooperation, instead of being wasted on political agendas and competitive strategy.

Happy people love themselves, and care more for others and the environment. Everyone benefits when more people are happy. Happy people care and give more (to society) than they take. Conversely, unhappy people cause more harm; they also take more from the world than they are able to give.

For example, many victims of society turn to crime because they are not happy with their life. Instead happy people are grateful and compassionate.

Everyone has the capability to be happy regardless of economy, culture, physical disability, education or intelligence. Not everyone in the world can be a billionaire, but every person can support real global evolutionary progress by learning to be happy.

Where to find Happiness

Happiness is the state of total wellbeing.

The route to happiness is internal. The outcome is peace of mind. People and stuff around us may uplift our emotional state for a short time only. Sustainable happiness is a state of mind and being.

A balanced lifestyle facilitates happiness. The essential components of total wellbeing are:

- Physical wellbeing including good physical health, a clean, natural and comfortable environment to support our survival;
- Mental & emotional wellbeing including the ability to deal with challenges, education and a positive empowering outlook;
- Social & cultural wellbeing including supportive family & friends, and a caring integrated community;
- Spiritual wellbeing including authentic creative expression, finding purpose, realising our potential and making a contribution to society.

Dr. David R Hawkins MD demonstrated that consciousness is related to level of happiness. Fear, shame and guilt correlate with a low level of consciousness, whereas love and joy indicate expanded consciousness. Spiritual techniques, including meditation, develop our consciousness.

LEVEL	INDEX	EMOTION
Enlightenment	700	Ineffable
Peace	600	Bliss
Joy	540	Serenity
Love	500	Reverence
Reason	400	Understanding
Acceptance	350	Forgiveness
Willingness	310	Optimism
Neutrality	250	Trust
Courage	200	Affirmation
Pride	175	Scorn
Anger	150	Hate
Desire	125	Craving
Fear	100	Anxiety
Grief	75	Regret
Apathy	50	Despair
Guilt	30	Blame
Shame	20	Humiliation

In a recent study at Wisconsin University, researchers found that people who meditate raise their happiness levels for a sustained period. This research suggests that the Buddhist concept of *Mindfulness*, and the ability to experience the present moment, enhances our quality of life.

The Index of Progress

The global index of progress – currently GDP - is the key determinant of human behaviour.

Every human being has a unique genetic code imprinted in their DNA. This code programmes our physical development. The world index of progress is like the operating system of planet Earth's computer. All human beings have their individual computer programmes linked into and supported by the world computer programme.

The most effective way to transform the world is to change the global index of progress. The pace of global transformation depends upon how quickly the new index is actually applied by our world leaders.

Our world's problems originate from our index of progress because it is based upon our man-made system of economics. The new happiness index is aligned with the natural evolution of this planet. Happiness is not a man-made concept; it is congruent with the inherent order of the universe.

NGOs and NFP organisations each have a specific mission to redress some aspect of the damage caused by using the GDP index. Examples include climatic change, cruelty to animals, genetic engineering, deforestation and campaigns against war.

So the time has come for every NGO and NFP organisation (and individual activists) in all areas to work together on the common cause – to establish the new happiness index for our beloved planet. Achievement of this single objective will eventually result in harmony.

Measuring Happiness

Happiness can be measured. *"Many good things can be measured and happiness is definitely one"* says Finance Minister of Bhutan, Lyonpo Yeshey Zimba.

The Happiness Index may adopt the same scale as that used by Dr David Hawkins. The scale is from zero (self-loathing, despair and suicidal feelings) to 700 (enlightenment).

The Total Happiness Index is the statistical average reading of the world population. Every human being influences real progress. Therefore The Total Happiness Index should take account of everyone. GDP takes no account of economic distribution; 12% of the world consumes 60% of the resources.

There are many ways to measure happiness. One practical way is to use an online multiple-choice questionnaire. An example is The Steen Happiness Index (www.authentichappiness.org).

Until the Total Happiness Index (THI) is the dominant progress indictor, it may be used in tandem with economic indicators. It is likely that GDP will decrease as the THI takes off.

PART II.
trickSTER TALES

CHAPTER 5

TRICKSTERS IN BUSINESS

MONKEY BUSINESS IN SOUTHEAST ASIA

Counterfeit Bank Notes

Ron paid 5,000 US dollars (in dollar bank notes) for ten computers. His first mistake was to pay for them in advance without any security. After ten days he had still not received the computers as promised, so he asked for a full refund. Ron received his money back and happily marched to his bank to deposit the money in his account.

The bank teller took one glance at the notes and immediately telephoned the police. The police arrested Ron for using counterfeit notes. The case was investigated and the person who paid Ron was sent to prison. It took Ron six weeks to be cleared of any involvement in the crime.

If you receive a large number of bank notes—for whatever reason—check them to ensure they are not counterfeit. If you have any doubts, go to your bank with the payer. It is usually more secure to receive payment by bank draft (a cheque drawn, signed, and stamped by a reputable bank on the bank's own cheque).

Creative Accounting

Brian, 68, from New Zealand purchased a café in Chiang Mai to supplement his retirement income. He was lured into the deal by the offer of low rent and expected earnings of US$ 1,000 per month. According to the seller's financial representations he would recover his investment within two years, which is normal.

Brian relied upon the seller's representations, which were supported by his business broker. The broker acted as the seller's intermediary without questioning the financial information. Brian did not seek independent advice, despite his Thai girlfriend's warnings about it being *"bad business"*; neither did he conduct any due diligence.

Within one week of the business transfer, Brian realised he had made a big mistake and decided to sell out as quickly as possible. He calculated that he needed to sell twelve cups of coffee per hour to achieve his target profit; he was only selling two cups per day (during peak season).

It took Brian over ten months to sell the loss-making business at a fraction of the price he bought it for. He had established a limited company to obtain a work permit he did not need because his girlfriend managed the café. Brian could have saved himself over 15,000 US dollars if he had researched the business properly.

Caution: Many sellers have no financial information about their business to offer buyers; others maintain three sets of records (one real account for themselves, plus manipulated accounts for the tax authorities and business investors).

The Fly-by-Night Bar

Chris, from Cardiff, was offered the opportunity to buy his favourite bar and restaurant. The sale price of $12,500 included a goodwill premium, music system, pool table, bar furniture, and stocks of beer and whisky. Chris accepted the offer.

Chris did not have a Thai partner, so he agreed with the selling tenant, David, to take over the existing lease, leaving it registered in David's wife's name. Neither Chris nor David mentioned the actual transfer of ownership to the landlord. Chris willingly paid David the asking price for the bar.

Within ten days of transfer of ownership, Chris was approached by the Thai landlord, who wanted to know who he was and why he was running the bar on his premises. When the landlord realized that his real lessee had transferred ownership of the business without his permission, he cancelled the lease on the spot. The next day the landlord instructed contractors to demolish the building.

Chris lost over $12,500 within three weeks of buying the bar because he did not negotiate a valid lease with the landlord or obtain legal advice. Chris and David were wrong and the landlord was understandably angry. Naturally, the landlord is eventually likely to hear about any change of business ownership because people talk.

The Dodgy Franchise

Tom paid $45,000 for a real estate property franchise covering northern Thailand. He met the (foreign) franchisors, who were extremely friendly to him. However, after paying the franchise fee to his franchisors, they refused to visit his new office in Chiang Mai and they would not return Tom's phone calls. Shortly after furnishing and equipping his new office, Tom broke his leg and then he decided to *"throw in the towel."*

Tom discovered that the franchisors were really tricksters—after paying them for a brand which had accumulated *"more bad-will than goodwill."* They had made false claims about their credentials and business history; and they owed money to numerous people in Thailand and overseas.

Research your franchisors thoroughly. Meet other franchisees and find out how their franchise is performing, and how much support they receive from the franchisor. It is positive if the franchisees respect their franchisor; conversely, if franchisees are resentful of their franchisor, do not proceed with the purchase.

Bogus Landlords

Steve agreed a lease for premises to operate a restaurant. Steve is cautious by nature, so he took both a Thai lawyer and his Thai representative to validate the lease.

After the lease was signed by both parties, he asked his lawyer whether he had checked that the landlord owned the property. The lawyer said that he had done so in front of his Thai representative.

Two weeks later, Steve discovered that the landlord was actually a lessee and not the owner of the property. The lawyer had accepted the lessee's verbal statement that he had *"forgotten to bring the property registration documents to the meeting."* Without agreement by the real landlord, Steve had no security of tenure over the lease term.

Do not sign a lease until you have evidence in writing that the person purporting to be the landlord actually owns the property. Check the landlord's personal ID card. Ensure that the landlord's name on the lease is exactly the same as that on the ID card and property registration document.

Defunct Businesses for Sale

Sometimes sellers attempt to present their business as a going concern after they have ceased trading. They manipulate the truth in order to justify asking for a premium for goodwill. Businesses which have ceased trading are usually sold for the nominal value of the second-hand assets.

Typically the seller would plan some activity to coincide with the prospective buyer's meeting. Bar or restaurant owners may ask their friends and family around to a party with a promise of free drinks. Therefore buyers are advised to make *"surprise"* visits to the seller's business to see how many customers there are at different times of the day, week, month or year.

TRICKSTER TALES FROM THE PHILIPPINES

Each region of the Philippines has its trickster: for example Juan or Suan of the Tagalogs and the Kapampangans; Juan Usong (Osong) of the Bicolanos; Juan Pusong of the Visayans and Sulu; Pilandok of the Maranaos.

The Visayan Juan Pusong has been described deceitful, dishonest and often cunning (Maxfield and Millington 1906: 107) and as 'a scampish young Filipino trickster and swindler in notorious escapades, and whose practical jokes are always amusing, frequently off-color, sometimes obscene, but rarely villainous' (Hart and Hart 1966: 315). Favorite tricks of these characters are as follows:

For some offense, Juan is arrested and trapped in a cage with intent to throw him into the sea after five days. Before expiry of that period, he is able to trick someone (typically a prince or nobleman) into exchanging places with him by saying that he was imprisoned because the King wanted him to marry the Princess and he is not worthy of her. The nobleman takes Juan's place and ends up being drowned. Later Juan returns from the sea and reports to the astonished King. So the King asks to be thrown into the sea. The King's request is granted and Juan becomes King.

Some tricksters possess unique characteristics. For example, Posong, trickster of Sulu, has a penchant for tricking the Sultan, and his exploits usually involve having illicit sexual relations with the Sultan's wives and other close relatives. An explanation is offered by a collector of Posong stories, *"The Posong stories are set in old Sulu, when the Sultan reigned autocratically"* (Nimmo 1970:

185). It would seem then that the tricks played on the Sultan are based upon a subconscious desire to get revenge on the figurehead.

The human trickster, Pilandok, is unique to the Maranaos, for the Tausug Pilanduk is an animal character, like the Malaysian Pelanduk, from whom the name, Maranao Pilandok, is derived.

The Malaysian Pelanduk, or Sang Kanchil, is a mouse-deer and counterpart of the animal trickster, Turtle. It should be noted, however, that the adventures of the Malay Pelanduk include marriage to a woman and transformation into a man (Yaapar 1977: I, 162). It would seem that it is in the human form that Pelanduk was transmitted to the Maranaos, because the Maranao Pilandok is always a human trickster, never an animal.

Two adventures attributed to both the Malay Pelanduk and the Maranao Pilandok are:
- Beating the Sultan's gong: Tiger is made to strike the 'gong' (a hornet's nest) with tragic consequences.
- Wearing the Sultan's 'belt' (snake): Tiger is tricked into wearing the sawa (snake) around its waist, and the creature nearly strangled him.

Trickster, Guatchinango, plays different tricks. In Guatchinango tales, the trickster is a sharp, shrewd swindler and knave. The tricks that Guatchinango and his kind play invariably involve cheating his victims of their money. For example, Guatchinango inserts two silver pesos into the rectum of his lean horse and sells him for a large sum as a money-dropping animal. The gullible buyer becomes impoverished and his wife dies of disappointment, while Guatchinango escapes to a distant place where he enjoys his ill-gotten wealth (FLPF 1058, Iloc.).

Other Guatchinango tricks include:
1. Selling a magic life-restoring whistle or flute.
2. Selling a magic hat which pays for anything purchased at any store or restaurant (FLPF 740).
3. Selling a magic frog whose movements reveals where money has been buried (FLPF 912).
4. Trickster Juan Pusing pretending to be dead to get money (FLPF 430).
5. Selling *"prophet powder"* which turns out to be bottled excrement (FLPF 605).

The Philippines also offers a generous supply of tales about numskulls and fools. These tales of stupidity are an endless source of merriment in any gathering. Incidentally, the most common folktales involve Juan Tamad or Juan Loco. Not surprisingly, Fansler found more tales about Juan than any other folktale hero.

Juan the Fool (FPT 49) is a Bulacan Tagalog tale which recounts the following madcap adventures of Juan:
1. Mother tells Juan to choose a quiet wife, so Juan brings home a dead woman.
2. Mother says: "Those who smell bad are dead". However, Juan's mother smells bad, so Juan buries her.
3. Juan smells bad to himself, so he floats down the river on a raft of banana trunks.
4. Robbers find Juan, appoint him their housekeeper, and tell him to keep quiet. When the rice he is cooking starts bubbling noisily, he breaks the pot to silence it.
5. Juan is sent to market to buy new earthenware pots and crabs, so Juan strings the pots on rattan to carry them

more easily. Then he released the crabs in water and told them to go home, ahead of him.

6. Robbers planning a robbery told Juan to go under the house to "case out the joint". His instructions were, "If you feel something hot, it's a man; if it is cold, it is a bolo". A warm lizard drops on him and Juan shouts out: 'Tao! Tao!,' which means "Man!" So the robbery is foiled.

In a Pangasinan tale, entitled *"The Seven Crazy Fellows,"* seven crazy fellows go out fishing. When they are ready to return home, they count themselves, but the counter forgets to count himself, so they think that one of their party has drowned. However an old man corrects them and leads them away.

In the forest, one fool hangs his hat and bag of rice on the antlers of a deer, thinking it is a branch of a tree. Inevitably, the deer runs away with his possessions.

One of the fools, who is sent to fetch some water from a well, sees his reflection in the water and nods to it. The reflection nods back, so the fool jumps in the well and drowns.

One fool cooks chicken without removing the feathers.

One fool who was asked to keep flies off the face of sleeping old woman, struck a fly on the nose of the lady, killing her. As they carry the corpse to the church, it falls off the flat coffin. The fools carry a live old woman and place her in the coffin, thinking she is the woman they are to bury, The lady's husband, hearing her cries, shouts to her that the fellows are just teasing her. The priest buries the living woman. When the crazy fellows return home, they discover the original corpse and think they are being chased by her ghost. They run away in different directions and end up scattered all over Luzon.

TRICKSTERS OF THE ROAD

Trickster of the Road drives according to his own rules. Road Trickster is color blind, so be careful at the traffic lights. Red lights are green to Road Tricksters, a bit like red flags to bulls.

Traffic signals render new meaning to Road Tricksters. When motorists indicate a left turn, the trickster interprets the signal as an invitation to overtake on the left hand side. Likewise, a signal to turn right is interpreted as *"Please overtake me on the right hand side"*.

Road Trickster's traffic signaling is often confusing. If Trickster indicates a left turn, this means that he may turn left or right; and there's a reasonable chance he will drive straight ahead or even reverse.

The Road Trickster is incapable of driving when he is sober because that's when he's asleep. Trickster attaches new meaning to *"drinking and driving"* since he actually drinks as he drives.

The Road Trickster uses his horn liberally – to attract attention of attractive ladies on the road. Road Trickster loves to arrange dates with attractive motorists whilst driving.

Road Trickster occasionally dresses up as a policeman and collects fines from motorcyclists who fail to wear safety helmets. Afterwards he drives with his bounty to play with his girlfriends – the girls who love men who wear uniforms. Road Trickster is easy to identify; he usually drives with up to four ladies (and a dog) riding pillion with him.

TRICKSTERS OF THE PUBLISHING INDUSTRY

Do you have a book you want to get published? If so, read this chapter before proceeding. Although writing (and getting published) is highly rewarding, there are many rogue publishers and other pitfalls to avoid.

Chiang Mai attracts many expats who want to enhance their quality of life. So Chiang Mai is host to many free-lance writers, software developers, photographers, artists (and con-artists), website designers, documentary makers and musicians from around the globe.

Many of the creatives gravitate towards the Writers' Club in the city centre. The bar was founded by ex-journalist and editor, Bob Tilley, and his charming Thai wife. The Writers' Club offers a relaxed ambience for media types to gossip in a congenial environment.

In Bob Tilley's interview for the business guidebook, *How to Establish a Successful Business in Thailand*, he comments that every successful bar is based upon a concept or theme. Bob's concept for the Writers' Club was imported from Eastern Europe where he found his model pub.

Another popular meeting place for *"scribblers"* and *"wordsmiths"* is The Writers' Group which convenes on Thursday evenings. The Writers' Group is one of the interest groups formed by the Chiang Mai Expats' Club. The purpose of these meetings is to encourage and support writers in their quest for literacy.

The Writers' Group attracts some talented writers. Although established writers do not usually attend, there is a committed core of wordsmiths who enjoy reading excerpts of latest creations to the group, and sharing constructive feedback with their fellow scribblers.

But be forewarned that writers are egotistical animals. Some two or three voices dominate the majority of the proceedings at the Writers' Group. Also, perhaps surprisingly, the group consensus leaned towards bigotry. One meeting was monopolized by a discussion about whether to ban spiritual people from their meetings.

The only regular member of the Writers' Group who has a book published is literary itinerant, Mo Tejani. Mo Tejani wrote *"Chameleons' Tales"*, which was published by Paiboon Publishing in 2006. Unfortunately Mo Tejani's book did not perform well according to sales numbers; but his book was nominated for a literary award.

Any aspiring author should consider benefiting from the free support offered by writers' groups which are located in most cities worldwide. The weakness of the Chiang Mai Writers' Group is its lack of focus upon getting manuscripts published. However, the constructive feedback and literary guidance offered is helpful.

I met Benjawan Terlecky, the founder of Paiboon Publishing, at Mo Tejani's book launch party, which was hosted at Bob's Writers' Club in 2006. Benjawan looked supremely elegant in her yellow summer dress.

I introduced myself to Benjawan and I told her that I had several short stories I wanted to get published.... would she be interested? (pause). But Benjawan seemed to be more interested in my experience as a franchise manager and business broker with Sunbelt Asia.

127

Benjawan registered her family publishing company in California, though the business is operated in Bangkok by her brother, Somchai. Today Paiboon Publishing boasts a portfolio of over 35 titles, including Thai language dvds, dictionaries and guidebooks.

Benjawan and her American husband, Nicolas, know how to work hard and play hard. The couple are avid Latin dancers and they regularly visit the wonders of the world. Their business supports an honorable lifestyle; their focus is not just money.

The following afternoon I received a phone call from Benjawan. She asked me whether I would be interested in writing a business guide book? I said I thought it sounded like an interesting project, so I would *"give her offer serious consideration."* At that time I was *"under-employed"* and keen to get a book published externally (rather than self-published).

A few days later I told Benjawan that I would be delighted to write the business guide book for her. Immediately after my trip to The Philippines in August 2006, I started writing the business guide book. I completed the first draft within four months. However I was risking my time because I had no publishing contract, and no advance of royalties or expense budget.

I was writing a guidebook without any clear guidelines or instructions. However the publishers had already published *How to buy Land and Build a House in Thailand* by Philip Bryce and *Retiring in Thailand*. Few publishers do offer guidelines for authors other than submission criteria which are often displayed on the publishers' websites.

128

Some publishers assert their own guidelines; for example, Bangkok Books reject any manuscript which mentions the Thai monarchy.

I met Benjawan and Nicholas in Chiang Mai in January 2007. I presented my first draft to them in the lobby of the Lanna Hotel. Obviously I was concerned that my manuscript could be rejected, thereby rendering four months of wasted work. I sensed that Benjawan was experiencing trepidation herself, seemingly psyching herself up to view a sample page.

After a cursory review of several pages of my manuscript, and a visit to the hotel bathroom, the mood transformed; Benjawan took me on a guided tour of Paiboon Publishing's contract. Within twenty four hours I was clutching onto a signed publishing contract. From that day onwards I believed in Buddha.

We decided upon the book title, *"How to Establish a Successful Business in Thailand"*. Some people say the title is too long, but this title conveys what is essential; *"How to"* means it is a guidebook, and *"Successful Business in Thailand"* means working with good Thai people at the front end of the operations.

During the following three months, I worked extensively with Nicolas Terlecky, the company's Vice President (renamed 'President of Vice' by Paiboon's graphic designer, Gordon Morton). Nicolas was extremely helpful during the editorial and re-writing process; he even provided some appropriate photographs to complement the text.

I also spent several weeks spending a lot of time with Gordon Morton who designed the book cover and typeset the *"guts"* of the publication. Gordon forewarned me several times that upon completion of the job we would not be on talking terms. I must compliment Gordon on his highly developed prophetic powers because I have not seen him since publication.

A sense of humor is prerequisite for working in the publishing industry. When one of my female friends visited Gordon's photography studio, he offered to take her photograph. *"Don't worry,"* he said, *"you will look great because I am a wizard with Photoshop software!"*

My business guidebook gained the abbreviated title of *"H2E"* (for *"How to Establish"*). One of the most important chapters in the book was *"Profiles of Successful Business People"*. Of course my challenge was to select appropriate businesses – that means legal businesses which would still be trading at least two years later.

Since writing H2E my beliefs about what is a successful business have changed. My original criteria for a *"successful business"* were sustained profitability and conformity with Thai law. The publisher, Benjawan, asked me to include more *"healthy businesses"* instead of including too many bars. Few of the farang yoga businesses operate legally (with work permits) so, instead, I selected Oasis Spa.

Under my revised criteria for a successful business, the operation should reflect the authentic nature of the owner; and the underlying intention of the business owner should be positive (to enhance the community somehow). Today I would reject any slimy, manipulative, cheating, or highly stressed business owners.

130

The process of interviewing highly successful – or highly stressed – business owners interested me. Each subsequent meeting with the business owners would reveal something of interest. Certain gems which I unearthed were too hot to publish; and on one occasion I was accused of suggesting that my interviewee had murdered a member of his family.

Several *"successful business people"* asked me not to publish their profile after several meetings of recorded interviews and hours of transcription. Many business people in Thailand live in fear of their business being copied; and many foreign businesses – and the Thai wives of the farang business owners – try to hide their profitability because jealous competitors can be callous.

Philip Bryce, the author of Paiboon's *"How to Buy Land and Build a House in Thailand"*, may be wise to adopt a pseudonym. Philip chooses to remain anonymous, though he receives many online enquiries from his guidebook which result in lucrative building project management jobs.

I decided to hold the book launch of H2E at The Writers' Club in Chiang Mai. I arranged complimentary food and wine at the event. I sent press releases to the local magazine publishers. That evening I performed my own breakeven analysis on the party's book sales. I needed to sell twenty copies to break even. I actually sold five copies of H2E at the launch party.

I witnessed one of the book sales to a travel writer. *"I probably won't bother to read it,"* he said, *"I am just buying it for my collection!"* Then he asked me how many copies I had sold. *"I've lost count,"* I replied.

Meanwhile my Thai girlfriend was being *"hit upon"* by several drunken farang; and my friend Jeannie, who has a British father and Thai mother, was accused of being a *"half-chaste"* by one drunken farang. Had I unwittingly hosted an event with free booze and food for the local alcoholic *"sexpats"* who had no interest in business guidebooks whatsoever?

Anyone considering a launch party for their new book should be advised not to expect any economic return from the event. Just write off the minimal cost of around five thousand Thai baht (one hundred pounds Sterling in July 2007). Invite your good friends and the press. And keep your Thai wife away from offensive sexpats who gravitate towards free wine.

Paiboon Publishing is a very well managed and ethical publisher. The management of Paiboon – Benjawan, Nicolas and Somchai - is personable and reliable. Benjawan and The President of Vice usually visit their *"stable of authors"* during their annual world tour from California. I sometimes refer to their style of business as *"holistic"*, which means that it's conducted with integrity.

Naturally I am biased, but I believe H2E is an excellent guidebook. The book was positively reviewed by the English language media throughout Thailand. The value in H2E lies in my investigative reporting and writing skills – not in my own ability to build a big business. Ironically, my personal finances floundered during this project, but Thailand's prominent business owners – including David Frost who is profiled in the book - say that H2E is well-written, interesting and comprehensive.

Many writers who get their books published experience post-publication blues. It's similar to post-natal depression; except with the added disillusionment of having your girlfriend propositioned for a short-term encounter during the launch party. The lingering questions post-publication are *"what's next?"*

I would advise any writer to take a proper holiday before launching into another project. Don't worry about the next project! I fell into this deadly mantrap and I vow to avoid this mistake in future.

Immediately I launched myself into an e-book project.

On 25 July 2007 I signed a contract with an online travel website called EA.com (not the real name) to write an e-book entitled *"How to Make a Living in Paradise"*. I heard that EA.com was eliciting manuscripts through a friend of mine.

E-books tend to be much shorter than printed books. Typically an e-book contains 10,000 to 30,000 words (average: 15,000 to 20,000 words). Printed books usually exceed 60,000 words. It is possible to write one or more e-books each month. Another benefit of writing e-books is that the royalties are usually four to five times higher (per unit sold) than that offered by traditional printed book publishers.

Short specialist technical guides are suited as e-books. Usually buyers want access to specific information immediately. Electronic guides typically retail for between US$5.00 and US50.00. My e-book, *How to Make a Living in Paradise*, retailed for US$20 and the author receives 40% of each copy sold.

I completed the manuscript for the e-book within six weeks and submitted it immediately to the online travel publisher for editing and uploading onto their website. Five months later I had not heard of any progress from the publisher, so I asked Steve Hogan, the company's managing director, for an explanation. Steve Hogan's email response (dated 30 December 2007) follows:

Hello Philip,

First, I apologize. It is my fault, as I am the owner of EA.com.

I am having a tremendous amount of trouble with every aspect of my company. Nothing is being completed by anyone on my staff. Some projects are years behind schedule, and when I complain the only things I hear are promises. I have, or once had, a multi-million dollar network that could have become one of the great website networks. Now, at the age of 67 I am losing every shred of hope that I will ever have anything. I suspect that my entire network is about to crash. Not one project that I have put in motion has been completed.

What I suggest you do is find a website, or publisher that cares about you and your writing. I care, but I cannot be twenty people. The essence of the problem is that I am not a programmer, and do not understand the intricacies of programming, so I am at the mercy of those who can program. If I could program I would have a website that functioned. As it is, I have nothing and am totally without hope that I ever will have anything.

Nobody gives a shit that I am 67 and have been waiting almost five years for the completion of a very wide number of much needed developments that were necessary for the evolution of my internet network. Soon I will be dead. But before that happens, I will take the goddamned website off the internet and erase it. If I could convey to you the extent of my dreams and plans, and the promise that my website network might have had you would be dumbfounded that my company has failed. But when one is handcuffed by ones lack of a mechanic, it doesn't matter if one is the best pilot in the world; without a mechanic, the plane won't fly.

As you said, my coordinator continues to make excuses for delays, but nothing actually gets done. That is the total essence of what I am faced with.

My sincere apologies for the lack of respect paid to you by my staff. I respect you, your writing, and your efforts. If I could be twenty people your e-book would be online. As it is, I doubt that it ever will be. It is my fault that you have been poorly treated, I am the owner, and I'll take the blame.

Steve Hogan

I wonder whether the above farcical letter is used as a standard template for all EA.com's online complaints. Perhaps Steve Hogan just inserts the aggrieved author's name after his salutation before hitting the *"SEND"* button.

Within ten weeks of Steve Hogan's claim of desperation, I received notification that my e-book was online – that's over nine months after I submitted the manuscript to EA.com. By comparison, Paiboon Publishing completed the editing, graphic design and layout, and printing of the book within five months.

EA.com's excuses for the delays were fantastic. The e-books coordinator, Jelly, advised me that her staff were being redeployed to other departments. On 15 February 2008 I received an email notifying me of Jelly's motorcycle accident and that she would be in hospital. Here is a copy of the email:

Hello Philip,

This is to inform you that Jelly was involved in a road accident earlier today. She is in hospital pending release tomorrow we think.

I do not want to allocate her duties at this time until I have more information and a better indication of when she will be back at her desk. I will evaluate this on Monday and advise you of the situation.

Naturally I sent Jelly a *"Get Well"* e-card.

I received notification of twelve sales of my e-book between 22 May 2008 and 3 November 2008. Then, after my request for payment and several reminders, finally I received payment of the royalties of US$96 by Western

Union (from Argentina) on 5 February 2009. Although the 3,300 Thai Baht received represented the hardest-earned cash, I felt triumphant as the bank cashier handed me the crisp banknotes over the counter.

I estimate that if I include my administrative time spent corresponding with EA.com, I invested a total of 130 hours in this project. To date, therefore, my e-book has returned just 25 Thai baht per hour. But don't forget, 25 baht is still enough to buy a noodle dish in *The Land of Smiles*.

Perhaps I have been too harsh on the ageing Steve Hogan's EA.com. They produced an excellent e-book from my manuscript. Fortunately I didn't sign an exclusive publishing contract with EA.com, so I can sell the publication on thousands of websites.

Since January 2009 I received a further two sales of my ebook, and in May I received an email from one of EA.com's employees called Pierre. Below is a copy of the message:

Dear Author

I am writing to you to inform you that from the 1st June 2009 I am no longer the eBook manager for EA.com.

I have spent the last few months trying to streamline the ebook administration to maximize sales and thus your profits. However, my position with the company is now untenable and I have resigned.

It is sad for me because I have enjoyed the interaction with all the ebook authors and the opportunity to use my PR and marketing background to the benefit of both EA.com and yourselves.

There are several projects on which I am working and I hope that at some stage you would not be averse to my contacting you in order to develop some mutually beneficial business.

Any queries regarding your ebook(s) should be addressed to Lazarus at EA.com.

In the meantime thank you for your continued support of EA.com and I wish you all the best.

Pierre Dupont
BA in Advertising
Master of MKT

The above missive indicated internal scuffles within the cyber-empire of EA.com. The following email – entitled EA.com Boycott – provides cast iron evidence of the intra-company chaos.

Hi,

My name is Paul Swift. I am contacting all ebook authors who have at present, or had in the past, ebooks for sale on EA.com.

I am part of a group of former employees of EA.com and ebook authors organizing a boycott of the website. We are soliciting testimonies by ebook authors who were not paid the agreed upon fees for the sales of their ebooks. We know from our past employment with EA.com that many of the ebook authors were either never paid, or not paid for long periods of time.

If you were treated thusly, I encourage you to submit your testimony to me. It can be one or several paragraphs long stating in your own words your business dealings with EA.com. By submitting your testimony you will authorize us to publish it, along with your name and email address, in our upcoming website dedicated to boycotting EA.com.

Additionally you will be placed on our list of aggrieved former-employees and contributors. The boycott will not be lifted until EA.com has satisfied its debts to each and every person on the boycott list.

If you have been paid you can still voice your displeasure at EA.com for not paying their debts which led to this embargo and which will lead to diminished website traffic. Please voice your concerns that their actions will cause you loss of exposure and business! And if you really want to help us, suspend your ebook from EA.com until this matter is settled.

It is unfortunate that we must resort to a boycott. However, some of us have been waiting years for payment resolution which never comes. We do have volumes of promises, however. Unfortunately, one cannot eat a promise, and we feel this is the only way to pressure the owner of the corporation into paying us. As you know, this is a Panamanian corporation and there is no legal recourse to address their wrongdoings. So, we are left to present our case in the court of public opinion.

I look forward to hearing your feedback and, of course, to having you join us.

Best regards,
Paul Swift

I asked Paul Swift what was going on inside EA.com and I received the following account:

Hi Phil,

I worked in advertising for 2 1/2 years. I brought in over $330,000 to the website and/or the managing director.

They quit paying the Argentine staff for a long period, 6 months or longer, with promises to catch up if we'd just be patient. Eventually the managing director removed all of my paid advertisers' ads and replaced them with Google Adsense ads. Stopped paying me and removed all my means of selling ads, hmmm, I can take a hint.

So I quit. Tried getting put on a payment plan to receive my back pay but am told there's no money. I raise a fuss, now I'm told they don't owe me any money as I have no contract. EA doesn't give out contracts to their employees and now I know why.

I have tons of files and emails to backup my claims, so I make them freely. I figure that if EA wants my computer confiscated and my files made public I'll be only more than happy to oblige them. Come and get me! Me, I haven't two nickels to rub together much less money to hire a lawyer to fight the managing director in his backyard, in a Panamanian court.

> *I'm a 50% disabled US veteran living on my $540 a month pension. They bilked a female employee out of $3,000, she's a 100% disabled US vet supporting 2 children. There's a gag order around the website so if you ask Jelly I am sure she'll say she's been paid, as the threats are flying that anyone seen as collaborating with me won't receive a dime (how they can pay us less than they're paying us now is beyond me).*
>
> *So, any help you could give would be appreciated.*
>
> *Regards,*
>
> *Paul Swift*

After completing the manuscript for my e-book (at the end of August 2007), I started looking for another book publishing contract. In September 2007 I identified a publisher called Paysoon Books seemingly looking for new writers. Alarm bells should have rung – or maybe they did, but I was wearing ear plugs. I wanted to scoop another publishing contract as quickly as possible.

The managing director of Paysoon Books, Mr Bill Taylor, was extremely enthusiastic that we work together. We had several telephone conversations during which we brainstormed possible publication concepts. Eventually we agreed upon a guidebook about cross-culture relationships in Thailand.

Bill Taylor did not stop harassing me until my submission of the manuscript. Soon I discovered that Paysoon Books was a one-man operation. Bill Taylor was company director, managing director, sales and marketing executive, publisher, editor, graphic designer, proof reader, receptionist, personal assistant to the managing director and boy Friday. This revelation occurred when I phoned Paysoon's switchboard, to be answered by Bill at his local hospital where his wife was giving birth.

Actually the fact that Paysoon Books was a one-man operation didn't matter. But Paysoon's unwillingness to account for sales properly or pay royalties did bother me. Beware the tricksters of the publishing industry.

The moral of this story is *"Conduct due diligence on your publisher before signing any contract."* Eventually Bill Taylor agreed to rescind the publishing rights.

All's well that ends well. Paiboon Publishing and Fast Track Publishing are highly recommended publishers based in Thailand. If possible, always contract with publishers based in your country of residence.

CHAPTER 6

SPIRITUAL TRICKSTERS

THE LAND OF PHILIP

A few people – including my friend, Kayce - repeatedly asked me the question *"Why are you going to The Philippines?"* Eventually I got weary of the same question and I found myself replying *"because I like the name, Philip."* Anyway, the question deserves some consideration, so I spent any idle time – for example while lolling around airports or during bus journeys - analysing my motives, attempting to justify this trip.

My main motive for the trip was that I had to get out of Chiang Mai because somehow I found myself in a rut. In this dark hole, I found myself pursued by people I did not want to see. I was surrounded by friendly alcoholics at a time when I craved a puritanical lifestyle.

In my notebook I compiled a list of objectives for this three week stint. Here is my list:

1. To check out the faith healers as an investigative spiritual journalist (and I really wanted to witness an operation by a psychic surgeon with my own bare eyes)
2. To take a break from drinking beer because my social life was becoming dependent upon it
3. To meet Lorraine, my great friend from Australia, who agreed to meet me in The Philippines
4. To take *"timeout"* from my relationship … You know exactly what I mean, right?

143

Ultimately I was there to repair my mind, body and spirit after nine months working with lawyers. I was there for a new life, to purge my sins, to clean up my being from inside out.

The Road to Baguio

Shortly after my arrival at the new Low Cost Carrier Terminal (LCCT) at Clark International Airport, I queued for the first bus to Baguio, a small city in the mountains where many faith healers reside. I immediately sensed the friendliness of the Filipino people and their sense of fun.

The Filipino wicked sense of humour was flamboyantly conveyed in the colourful signs on the jeepneys (which are converted US jeeps used as plebeian taxis). Examples, worthy of note, are *Hi Babes*!, *The only Boy*, *Prince Charles*, *Guardian Angel*, *Dream Boy* and *Kiss me & Smile!* My favourite tagline, though, was *Ladies Choice*.

Welcome to Baguio!

Baguio is a magical city in the mountains and its atmosphere is commonly compared to Chiang Mai. I learnt that this city is a favoured destination for Filipino retirees and many people who work in Manila spend their weekends there. Naturally it's much cooler and rainier in Baguio than Manila.

I spent my first night in an English pub called The Red Lion, offering the only budget accommodation listed in my Lonely Planet Guide. The Red Lion is a charming watering hole offering a bottle of San Miguel beer for only US$0.50. Everyone was very friendly, so I was immediately introduced to the local alcoholic expatriates. Above the main wooden table was a sign reading *Der Tabul ov Nolige*. Now I was part of yet another family.

That evening I was offered the possibility of an English-teaching job. Baguio attracts many Korean students of the English language. I also met a newly arrived Canadian, Ted, who reckoned he could fix me up with a two-bedroom apartment for only US$100 per month. On my first night in Baguio, it seemed, I had found a job, a home and a social life; and there were many eager Filipinas willing to cook and clean for me.

Jun Labo & the Fake Healers

After two days of exploring the city I decided to visit a famous faith healer named Jun Labo. I read an article on the internet which primed me for the experience; since his role of Mayor of Baguio, he had been imprisoned in Russia for faking a surgical operation using pig's blood. Jun had also numerous ex-wives, so he probably enjoyed his power and social status.

I took a taxi to Jun Labo's mailing address, Nagoya Inn. [Nagoya is the Japanese city where one of Jun Labo's ex-wives used to live]. When I mentioned to the Filipino taxi driver that I wanted to visit faith healers, he responded *"Oh, you mean the fake healers?"* When a Filipino pronounces the word Fake, it sounds like Faith. Now I was quite doubtful of Jun Labo's authenticity.

On arrival at the Negoya Inn, I paid the taxi driver. As I watched the taxi drive away, it became apparent that the inn was derelict. I peered through a couple of the win-

145

dows to discover empty rooms. My loud knocks on the door failed to attract anyone's attention. In the courtyard stood several larger-than-life statues of swans and winged deities together with Jesus Christ and the Mother Mary. I thought this scene would be perfect for a surreal movie.

I started to walk back to the main road, and I noticed a young boy washing some dishes. I wondered whether the dishes contained human blood or pig's blood. I asked the boy where Jun Labo was. He ignored me, so I continued walking towards the road. *"Where are you from?"* the boy asked eventually. "England," I muttered while waiting for a taxi. My answer seemed to immediately unlock some secret code because instantly the boy remembered where Jun Labo was, and he even agreed to take me to visit him!

We walked down the main road and up a driveway on the right hand side. We arrived at what appeared to be a fortress. The gates in front of us were about fifteen feet high. We were greeted by the barking of savage Alsatians. Two tough-looking security guards unlocked the gates to let us in. The Alsatians gnashed their teeth at me while one of the guards walked to the main building. Shortly I was ushered into Jun Labo's house.

I entered the front door. I passed another statue of Christ the Man and more winged deities. The room in front of me was dimly lit. I was surprised to find the room packed with 24 Japanese students of mediumship (including an interpreter) and close disciples of Jun. I was immediately greeted by a buxom lady called Elizabeth. I discovered later that Elizabeth was a famous Filipina actress who co-facilitated and organised Jun Labo's healing seminars. I quickly realized that I had arrived on the third day of a two week seminar programme. I was invited to sit down and observe.

I listened to Jun Labo as he facilitated a psychic process. He is a short man, wearing tight black jeans and cowboy boots. I observed that he needed to take regular breaks to satisfy his nicotine habit. Having heard so many cynical accounts of *"fake healers,"* I was aware of my mounting scepticism, and at times I found myself chuckling to myself while I imagined Jun Labo in an advertisement for Marlboro cigarettes.

We were all invited to participate in a group meditation process. Elizabeth initiated the process by clicking the *"Start"* button of the CD player. I wondered whether the CD had been purchased from Amazon.com or a retail stall; so my mind was wandering. Elizabeth broke my day dream when she asked me to meet Jun Labo in his office.

I greeted Jun in his office, in the next room. He had a massive wooden desk with a prominent sign displaying his name above the word MAYOR. I introduced myself and told him I was thinking of enrolling on one of his seminars. He assured me that, although I had missed the first two days of the seminar, I hadn't really missed anything at all! Now was as good a time to enrol on the course as any, apparently. I summoned up the courage to ask the cost of the two week seminar programme. *"US$1,000,"* he answered. *"So the total cost is US$1000, is it?"* I asked cautiously. *"Per week"* was Jun Labo's answer.

I was reeling from a state of shellshock as it dawned on me that Jun was charging 24 people a sum of US$2,000 each for ten days *"work"*. The Filipino Marlboro Man earns US$48,000 for ten days work; almost US$5,000 per day in a "developing" country! Now I was carefully considering my position. I ruled out the option of enrolling on the course, but I was curious to learn more about his practises. So I told Jun that I would *"sleep on the decision about enrolling on the current seminar"* if he would let me stay for the remainder of the day's seminar. This way I would receive US$200 worth of seminar, gratis.

Suddenly Elizabeth interrupted our conversation. *"The exercise worked perfectly this time!"* she reported to Jun, bursting with joy. Jun patted Elizabeth's posterior; he had an expression of contained satisfaction on his face. I wondered what I had missed. Jun explained to Elizabeth about my situation, and they agreed to let me attend the rest of today's seminar without any obligation to enrol on the course.

I returned to the seminar. After a break, Jun Labo facilitated a process of astral projection. Jun Labo picked two volunteers (in true Army-style) for this exercise. They were assisted into a state of trance and asked to project themselves on the astral plane to each other's home. Both participants were asked to describe each other's house whilst in a trance. I was not convinced by the result; I thought Jun Labo was trying to make the description fit the reality. The audience clapped after successful completion of yet another magic circus trick.

Throughout the day I became more convinced that Jun Labo was neither sincere, nor authentic. He did not perform any surgery during that afternoon. Furthermore, some of his comments seemed inarticulate, like *"don't eat too much lunch, so the Holy Spirit can get inside you."* I sensed that he was trying to impress his audience rather than share something truly valuable. However, I did like Elizabeth's enthusiasm and style of facilitation; she really held the seminar together.

Most of the exercises either involved playing recorded CDs or facilitation by Elizabeth. Jun Labo dropped in occasionally, cigarette in hand, to keep an eye on his show. I met a couple of his devotees from the days when he really was a faith healer; a young boy of ten years old who claimed that Jun Labo was his Godfather. I also met his mother. This young boy was highly developed spiritually, as was his mother. He offered me an Angel Card reading. What a charming kid, he was!

As I left the seminar, I felt pity for Elizabeth and the devotees since they could have directed their energy towards a more worthy cause. I told Elizabeth I would call her if I decided to enrol on the course.

The Pranic Healers

On 4 August I discovered a Pranic Healing Centre. It was a very serene environment and I enjoyed chatting with the healers. I learnt that the system of Pranic Healing was established in The Philippines by the Master Choa Kok Sui, who is an engineer of Chinese ancestry. As a scientist, I was attracted to the system because it is highly structured and easy to understand. I enjoyed receiving a pranic healing session by Julios and his female colleague.

I experienced a Pranic healing treatment by two of the practitioners. They balanced my external energy field using crystals. They also measured the vibrational frequency of each of my chakras (or energy hubs) using crystal pendulums. I was suitably impressed by their treatment and I felt recharged afterwards. I also liked the professional structure of their training manuals and guide books.

The following day, my special friend, Lorraine arrived in Baguio so we went to Forest House restaurant for a celebratory meal. The next day we both visited the Pranic Healing Centre. This time, Lorraine had a healing treatment.

Back to Manila

Lorraine and I visited the home of another famous faith healer called William. However, we did not manage to catch the man at home. Apparently William loves collecting cars and drinking Jack Daniels whisky. These revelations possibly contributed to Lorraine's doubts about William's authenticity as a healer. We did not meet William on this trip.

We tried to make contact with the famous faith healer, Reverend Alex Orbito. Alex worked from his travel agency in Metro Manila. We arranged an appointment to meet him on Friday 11th August. We also received an invitation to meet a group of Reiki practitioners, known as the Soul Sisters, in Manila the following evening. So we arranged to get up early the next morning and board a bus to the big city.

The Soul Sisters

My contact with The Soul Sisters was Rosanna. I connected with Rosanna via a Google seach. We were

150

driven to an exclusive house in a secure compound, on the outsKurts of Manila. The house belonged to Lia, a sophisticated lady who is the editor of Manila's *High Society* magazine. Her house was beautifully designed and interior decorated to the finest detail.

There are five Soul Sisters, but one of them was unable to attend the party. The sisters were called Rosanna, Lia, Iris and Laya. Lia organised a delicious buffet of traditional Filipino cuisine. We all chatted and laughed. Apparently the Soul Sisters met once a month for a group Reiki session; their respite from the routine of work and the duties that go with being a wife in the hustle and bustle of crazy Manila.

The Soul Sisters expressed interest in our work, so Lorraine and I facilitated a group meditation. Although it only lasted for half an hour, it was a powerful group experience. Apparently some of the group participants heard water dripping from the ceiling onto the table. After the meditation we could not find any reason for the leak.

After the dinner party I felt my body preparing for my treatment with Alex. I needed to drink copious quantities of water. I was also aware of numbness in my hands. I sensed that my body was being purified in many ways.

The Real Thing

By Noon, when Lorraine and I arrived at Alex's offices, I had already drunk three litres of water. We waited for the lift to arrive, but it was stuck on the nineteenth floor and I desperately needed to use the toilet. The ten minutes we waited for the lift were painfully long. Eventually we found the travel agency and I was able to relieve myself.

The travel agency was nondescript. There were a few tatty posters advertising airlines pinned to the walls. The phones did not ring while we were there. There was a large plastic sofa for customers (or patients) to sit on. There were two girls working in the office for Alex. It seemed that the travel agency was a front for Alex's energy work. He always has a busy schedule and he is constantly travelling inside and outside his country.

I was very nervous indeed. The last time a doctor took a syringe full of my blood for testing, I passed out. So Lorraine (who had previously been operated upon by Alex) agreed to be treated first. I also explained that I only really wanted to observe an operation; I didn't need to be operated on myself! I suggested just a little energetic tune-up; an external spring-cleaning of my energy centres (or chakras). After all, there was nothing wrong with me!

The door opened. My God, it's Alex! My heart was working overtime now. Alex is a short middle-aged man. He is softly spoken, charming and humble. We are invited into a small room next to his *"travel agency"*. We chat for a while after introducing each other. Lorraine reminds Alex that their paths crossed some four years ago in India. Then Alex said a prayer and Lorraine was invited to lie down on the massage table.

Alex held some cotton wool and dipped it in water. Then he moistened an area on Lorraine's bare stomach. He recited more prayers and then suddenly I could see his hands penetrate Lorraine's body. I heard a squelching sound as his hands played inside Lorraine's body. Some blood dripped out of the open incision. I noticed that Lorraine remained completely calm; she even spoke to Alex in an even voice. Alex was picking black *"impurities"* out of Lorraine's body and placing them in a bowl.

Alex operated on Lorraine on her stomach as well as her back and both sides of her hips. I watched the operation in absolute amazement. I was tempted to take a photograph, but I stopped myself, thinking it would seem crass and disrespectful to Alex. He worked very quickly and efficiently. He closed up the incisions with ease, and there were only small scars remaining. Lorraine reported that the pains she had in her thighs stopped immediately after the surgery.

Now it was my turn! At this moment, I remember thinking that maybe my liver needed a cleaning. Anyway, I lay down on my back and Alex prepared for the surgical operation. I mumbled something about a *"little diagnosis and external tune-up,"* but I am not sure whether he heard me. Alex reported that I needed some surgery on my liver and bladder. *I knew I had drunk too many Singha beers!* I was thinking. I found myself conceding to the operation. I held Lorraine's hand like a baby.

I could hear the squelching noise as Alex pulled impurities out of my liver and bladder. I did not feel any pain whatsoever. The operation only took a few minutes, while I nearly crushed Lorraine's hand during my terror. I would not have been able to proceed with the operation without Lorraine. After the surgery I noticed I had two small scars, which remained with me for about one week. I felt overjoyed after the experience. The area around my stomach felt a bit sensitive for the following 24 hours though. This was a huge milestone in my life.

I purchased Alex's book *"Born to Heal."* I learnt many things about energy healing. Apparently Alex gets drained in the presence of negative or sceptical people; sometimes he is unable to operate in their presence. He confirmed that rich living and power corrupt his divine healing abilities; this explains what happened to Jun Labo. It's remarkable how being world-famous has not corrupted Alex; he is one of the most charming, humble and decent men I have met. Alex is a real faith healer; and someone suggested that there may be only 20 or so such people in the whole world.

The Return

The following day, Lorraine had to leave the country. Lorraine was staying in The Philippines unofficially because her flight to Manila was scheduled via Hong Kong. The weather conditions prevented the plane from landing in Hong Kong, so it flew direct to Manila. Lorraine was eventually allowed through Immigration, but they did not stamp her passport because entry was illegal according to international law. Anyway, she was allowed to leave the country without visiting a local jail!

For the following few days I was engaged in a total detox. Each day I drank over six litres of water. I had to plan my activities around toilets. I did not feel too safe in Manila, so I always carried an umbrella with a prominent spike at its foot. It might have been appropriate to wear a T-shirt displaying Clint Eastwood's words: *"Go ahead, Punk, Make my day!"* I was constantly hounded by touts trying to sell fake Rolex watches or Viagra. I noticed that most retail shops employed security guards carrying automatic machine guns. Manila is an edgy place, such a contrast to Baguio.

When I arrived back to Chiang Mai I did share my experiences with a couple of people. I quickly discovered that sharing these remarkable events usually resulted in alienation; they would say something like *"Sure, I believe you.... but it's impossible!"* Now that's a fair comment... after all, how could it be true?

THE MONK'S VANISHING CAP

Outside a village in Burma there was a derelict monastery which was rumored to be inhabited by evil ghosts. Everyone who visited the ruins was later found dead with all of their bones broken.

One day the village drunkard walked to the ruined monastery to enjoy his drink in peace. As he was drinking his toddy, an obese monk entered the room and asked him whether he could wrestle. Annoyed at being disturbed, the drunkard replied, *"Of course, I can wrestle, Sir!"*

So the fat monk insisted, *"Come and wrestle with me then!"* And so the fat monk and the drunkard wrestled. Although the drunkard used all the tricks of wrestling that he knew, they were to no avail because the monk's body was like a sack of potatoes and as slippery as a snake. Also, although the drunkard was huffing and puffing like a dragon, the monk's breathe was not disturbed. Gradually the drunkard realized that he was fighting a ghost of the monastery.

Eventually the drunkard was caught in a vice-like grip and his body was being beaten repeatedly by the monk. In desperation, the drunkard gripped with his hands the shaven head of the monk and, to his surprise, he felt a leather cap on the monk's head, although it was invisible to his eyes. He quickly snatched away the cap. At once the monk let go of his opponent and pleaded with the drunkard, *"Please let me have my cap!"*

The drunkard asked the monk why he should return his cap, *"Why should I? I need a new cap and now I have one!"*

156

The monk explained to the drunkard, *"This cap is a special vanishing cap which all ghosts need. Without my cap, I cannot disappear! And when the cap is taken away from us, we cannot snatch it back. So I must wait until you return it to me."*

The drunkard laughed, *"Ha! Ha! Your information is very useful. Now I can take you back home with me to be my servant for five years. After that time I will return your cap to you as reward for your loyal service."* However, the ghost was sullen and not in the mood for such jokes.

In desperation, the monk told the drunkard of seven pots of gold buried underneath the reception of the ruined building. *"Return my cap,"* said the monk, *"and I will show you where to dig for the gold."*

By now the drunkard was feeling intoxicated and lazy, so he told the poor ghost to dig for the riches. After the ghost had unearthed the pots of gold, the drunkard commanded the ghost to carry the bounty for him. As they approached the village, the drunkard realized that the villagers would beat him if he forced a monk to carry his bags. So the drunkard returned the cap to its rightful owner, and the drunkard returned home alone with his riches.

THE ETHERIC HANGOVER CURE

The following invocation is a sure-fire way of over-coming habitual alcoholic abuse. Note, however, this manuscript is copyright-protected by international law, and each time you read this magical invocation you are indebted to the originator, the sum of $500. Phil Nicks will accept payment in cash, or exchange with surplus supplies of beer and whiskey.

THIS IS THE END OF THE LINE FOR ME....

Today I feel like shit. It's just another day of hangover, blurred vision, the feeling of a hedgehog attached to my contact lenses, blood-shot eyes, depletion, nicotine-stains, bloated belly, feeling fat and crippled, excessive layers of subcutaneous fat on my cheeks, feeling dumb, wasted, stu-pefied and that sickly odour of toxins, as I sweat it out of my body.

BUT TODAY I CHOOSE LIFE....

Today I choose health spas, aromatherapy toilet tissues, organic underwear, low-cholesterol vegan bean soups, tea tree up the bum, undocumented rigorous workouts, herbal steam hairspray, 10-gear racing hydrotherapy, clear and focused banana wraps, chakra-balancing festivals, tantric brainstorming symposiums, fair-trade genital acupuncture, triple yoga enhancement systems, multi-coloured harmon-ic pentagrams and multi-orgasmic urine therapy.

I, HEREBY RESOLVE....

I rescind any and all vows and contracts I have taken, anyone in my body has taken, and anyone within my genetic and spiritual lineage has taken, pertaining to:

*"I will give away all my power to short-time prosti-
tutes, long-time pimps, cigarette cartels, commission-
craved government officials, organized crime syndicates,
purveyors of low-grade ethanol, sundry depressive and
pharmaceutical drug barons."*

I NOW DECLARE THESE VOWS AND CON-
TRACTS NULL AND VOID in this incarnation and all
incarnations, across time and space, all parallel realities,
parallel universes, alternate realities, alternate universes,
all planetary systems, all source systems, all dimensions
and the Void by the force of Grace, the essence of Purity,
the power of Faith and the decree of Victory...

Please release all structures, devices, entities, parasites, orientations or effects associated with these vows
and contracts NOW!

THE BIRTH OF THE PUNK MONK

Evolution is not possible without the opposing force of corruption. Impurity is the prerequisite for the alchemical process of purification.

Temptation to corruption - or The Shortcut - places short-term material reward above the journey - or The Work - which brings wisdom. Therefore corruption is a form of spiritual disease which sacrifices wisdom in favor of ego-gratification.

"The perfection of our essence can be realized only if consciousness is altered and transmuted from the base, normal level (lead) to a higher spiritual level (gold). Whereas the aim of mysticism is union with God; the goal of alchemy is the inward process of perfecting the individual and immortalization of the Soul."
- Bette Jo Benner

Enoch and Lucy Fox live in a stately residence near Guildford, Surrey. Enoch Fox is a slight freckled dentist with copper wire hair and the complexion of a frozen chicken. Enoch prides himself in his exactitude – his trousers always boast a stiffly pressed crease; and his leather shoes, the military sheen of the most disciplined officer.

Enoch has an angelic-looking wife called Lucy, a reliable Volvo saloon and an obedient black labrador called Brutus. The Fox family has a well-tended garden of weeping willows, somber rhododendrons and azaleas. In springtime, the garden is speckled with innocent-looking snow drops, crocuses and daffodils.

Lucy's remit is to portray the sad self-sacrificing martyr, the loyal housewife and humble servant of Enoch. Enoch picked her up during her nubile prime, saving her from her alcoholic parents and heinous suitors. Enoch constantly reminded Lucy how lucky she was to be part of a family of genuine upper-middle class gentry – and all she had to do was *"sit pretty"* and follow his dictates.

The Fox residence had an aura of order extending beyond the hawthorn hedges which marked its perimeter. *"Everything has its place"* is Enoch's motto. The branches of each oak tree were allowed to extend so far – but should they cross Enoch's predetermined boundaries – their audacity would be met by Enoch's menacing chainsaw.

The time-warped family home was a museum of heir looms, antique furniture and a gallery of portraits of Enoch's descendents (as well as photographs of Margaret and Dennis Thatcher, and Sir Winston Churchill). The Fox family's coat of arms was displayed prominently above the mantelpiece in the smoking room which hosts the billiard table.

The tall spacious rooms were always chilly and filled with a composite odor of cigar smoke, polish and leather saddle soap. Lucy was resigned to being resident housekeeper, chambermaid and Enoch's personal assistant.

Enoch also employed Boy, a part-time gardener originally from Zimbabwe. The dyslexic Boy always greets his master obsequiously with a stutter, *"S-S-Sir, what can I d-d-do for you n-n-next?"* When taking leave, after completing of his duties, he would bow down humbly until he could see his reflection in Enoch's shiny boots.

The Foxes lead a structured life. On Friday evenings they visit their friends at the local pub called The Wheat Sheaf. On Saturday mornings they tend to their private botanical gardens; and in the afternoon they take Brutus for *"walkies."* On Saturday they would either attend – or host - a dinner party; and Sunday is strictly reserved for gardening, walking and teatime with Enoch's parents.

On Saturday morning Enoch parked his Volvo into the garage before carrying his recently acquired potted rhododendron shrubs into the back garden. He placed the plants on the lawn between the flower bed and the perimeter hedge. Enoch peered over the hawthorn hedge to survey his new neighbors.

Enoch clenched his teeth like a savage as he observed his neighbors in their native Pakistani attire, stepping into their four-wheel drive. *"Damn wogs, go back to Niggerland!"* he muttered as he contemplated the decline of what he regarded a decent neighborhood.

Enoch believed that the lifeblood of the British Empire was being sucked away by a rapidly growing population of chapatti-guzzling parasites. Enoch shook his head in exasperation; then suddenly his body seized as he focused on a critical patch of lawn: Enoch had spotted an audacious weed on his property.

Enoch placed his right hand inside the pocket of his Gortex jacket and pulled out a pair of rubber gloves. Then he slowly dressed his hands with the rubber ware, as if preparing for a surgical operation. Enoch knelt down onto the lawn and articulated, *"You don't belong here, do you? Now it's time for you to join your little friends."* He held the ragweed at its base between his thumb and index finger, and slowly lifted its roots out of the soil. Then he stood up and hurled the weed over the hedge into his neighbor's garden.

Enoch wheeled a barrowful of peat towards the potted plants as Lucy arrived back from her shopping trip. She rushed into the kitchen, armed with two heavily laden carrier bags of groceries. Enoch entered the kitchen as Lucy was loading the refrigerator with supplies.

"I managed to buy the book you wanted," Lucy said triumphantly. She handed a hardback publication to Enoch. The cover comprised a portrait of a well-groomed gentleman in military attire. The title was, *"Rudolf Hess ~ Biography."* Enoch stood motionless for a minute, gloating over his latest possession. His serene expression suddenly gave way to exasperation. *"What are we going to do about those bloody wogs next door?"* he asked. Lucy sighed as she placed the dog food in the corner cabinet.

Enoch returned to the garden after drinking a cup of his favorite Earl Grey tea. He always brewed his tea in a china teapot, insisting that nobody else knew the art. First, the pot needs to be warmed up by pouring hot water inside. *"It's an art"* reflected Enoch, *"and nowadays no-one has a damn clue about anything."*

Enoch returned his attention to the azaleas which were ready for planting. Just then, the neighbor's rottweiler began barking frantically. Enoch resolved to deal with the *"wretched animal"* if the local Council's Noise Pollution Unit would not respond to his official compliant to his satisfaction.

At four o'clock, Enoch retired to his sun lounge for a pot of Earl Grey tea and a gingerbread biscuit. The contentment which welled inside during his horticultural activities evaporated when a devastating seed thought – like a miniature nuclear missile – struck his entire being. His head collapsed into his palms as he pleaded that his *"inconvenient issue"* be resolved.

Enoch had always been repulsed by any form of bodily contact, the way of *"sissies and poufs"*. His mother was forcing him into a corner with her repeated demands for grandchildren. Enoch had promised his parents at least one grandchild, and he had built an extension to their house with her *"gesture of reciprocal appreciation,"* as she coined the phrase.

Enoch and Lucy slept in separate beds and their bodies had not made any form of contact since the wedding ceremony at St Peter's Church, four years ago. That afternoon, Enoch planted a cold scabby kiss on Lucy's innocent cheek – the final act of sealing the fiscal contract - for the entire congregation to witness.

For Enoch, having a wife was part of a squire's duty. If he took Brutus out on a country shooting trip with his old school friends, he would return with a couple of pheasants. All Enoch had to do was drop them on the floor of the porch. Lucy would pluck the feathers of the birds, and afterwards the Foxes would eat pheasant broth with wholewheat bread.

After sipping the final drops from his teacup, Enoch walked purposefully into his study. He switched on his computer and connected to the internet. Beside his personal computer lay a hardback publication entitled *"Practical Eugenics ~ How to customize your baby."* Enoch tapped the keywords *"sperm donor wanted"* into the Google search field. Then he started researching his options.

Enoch found a site – originally called *"Sperm Mart"* – which promised to deliver fresh sperm in an *"Immaculate Conception (IC) Toolkit"* within twenty minutes of inception. The charge for up to 20 milliliters of spermatozoa started at $100.00 (exclusive of handling and delivery fees). The product cost varies according the pedigree of the originator. For example, a budget of $100.00 (exclusive) would cover the cost of a local welder's sperm. But Enoch would have to pay $1,000.00 for the seminal secretions of a local aristocrat or Caucasian medical doctor.

Enoch smirked with joy as he scrolled through the categories of *"sperm providers."* He thought $100 was an absurd price for an unemployed Muslim's sperm. *"God, what's the world coming to?"* muttered Enoch.

At 9.00pm Enoch decided to order the pedigree spermatozoa of a local Caucasian aristocrat. The total fee of $1,450.00 included KY jelly, hypodermic syringe, instruction booklet, 24 hour telephonic customer support, and delivery guaranteed to be within thirty minutes of emission. Enoch paid online and printed out the transaction details and confirmation. Then he walked upstairs to have a little chat with Lucy about this matter.

After Enoch briefed Lucy of his online purchase order, he walked over to his bedside table and programmed his digital clock to sound an alarm at 9.30pm, the deadline for the delivery of spermatozoa. Then he lay on his bed clutching his biography of Rudolf Hess. Enoch noticed that he was unable to concentrate as his mind skated across the paragraphs of the Introduction.

Enoch was preparing himself for his role as father already. He was fulfilling his duty to his parents and society. The local community would respect him for seemingly passing on his pedigree genes to the next generation. *"Procreation is a messy business,"* mused Enoch, *"but we need to pass on the family name with dignity."*

At 9.15pm a high-frequency sound seemed to envelope the Fox residence. Concurrently, the property began trembling; and suddenly the lights faltered. Enoch and Lucy rushed over to the bedroom window to observe the intense light as a translucent UFO spaceship landed on the rear lawn.

The spaceship, which was circular and contained an equilateral triangle, covered the entire lawn. The Foxes were mesmerized by the spectacular sight of extraterrestrial technology. The alarm clock stopped at 9.15pm. They waited in awe, motionless.

Three extraterrestrial punks wearing bright multicolored Mohican hairstyles emerged from the spacecraft. The barefooted beings wore ripped blue jeans and vests, revealing otherworldly tattoos. The leader walked in front, carrying a package towards the house.

The doorbell rang five times. Enoch walked downstairs to open the door. *"We have a delivery of prime DNA from the planet, Chiron!"* announced the leader of the spaceship who introduced himself as Joe. His colleagues were called John and Jella. Enoch noticed that Joe's teeth were coated in plaque. Joe brazenly exclaimed *"We are the three wise men; and we have something for you!"* as he displayed a package bearing the words *"Immaculate Conception (IC) Toolkit"*. After Enoch signed the triplicate delivery note, the three extraterrestrial beings pushed past Enoch and alighted the staircase towards the master bedroom.

The clock read 9.15pm. John and Jella asked Enoch to sit down on his bed before sitting down on each side of him. Joe explained that he needed privacy with Lucy to *"take her through the motions, so-to-speak."* John and Jella exchanged a grin. Joe strolled into the guest bedroom with Lucy, still holding onto the IC Toolkit.

"Nice neighborhood!" commented Jella, smiling. *"Yes, but let's listen to some decent music while we are waiting. None of the classical bollocks, thanks! Let's play this!"* John suggested as he loaded a CD into the music centre. The lyrics, *"Teenage kicks, so hard to beat!"* lifted the somber mood of the Fox residence.

The sound of Lucy's giggles challenged the sound of punk music. *"What on Earth is going on?"* Enoch asked abruptly. *"Sounds like your wife is having fun, doesn't it?"* said Jella, grinning. The sound of giggling gave way to sighs of ecstasy and deep breathing. Then, as Lucy began shrieking with joy, Enoch fainted.

Enoch awoke at 7.15am with a splitting headache. He was lying on his bed, fully clothed. The memory of his experience – or dream – from the previous evening left

167

him frightened and confused. He noticed, to his horror, that Lucy's bed was empty and the bed sheets uncreased.

Enoch stood up and walked towards the guest bedroom. Slowly he turned the door knob and, hesitating, he peered around the door. Lucy was lying on the floor spread-eagled, wearing nothing other than an aura of divine contentment. Enoch wondered why she looked so different, so…..happy.

Enoch stammered, *"Darling, I think I had a nightmare last night,"* and walked out of the room awkwardly. He peered out of the window to observe the lawn, which looked the same as usual. Enoch was worried that he might find evidence that his memory of the previous evening was real. He stared at his music centre and then summoned enough courage to press the Eject button. The music system curtly spat out a CD entitled *Teenage Kicks* by The Undertones. Enoch's mood sank into despair.

"Darling, where is the IC Toolkit?" Enoch called. Lucy said she did not know where it was. Enoch searched frantically for the box containing a phial of pedigree seamen, without success. However, on a walnut desk – within spitting distance of the front door – he identified a copy of a Sperm Mart delivery note for the IC Toolkit, signed by him at 9.15pm last night.

Enoch was seething with rage. He grabbed the delivery note and identified the Customer Service Hotline. Underneath the hotmail number was a tacky tagline: *"Coming Quickly to Our Valued Customers!"*

Enoch dialed the hotline number and listened to a recording of the Monty Python song, *"Every Sperm is Sa-*

168

cred!" followed by an automated response, *"For new accounts, press one; For re-orders, press two; For payment options, press three; For details of your success story, press four; and if you want to be entered into this month's prize draw, press five. Have a great day and an ever greater immaculate conception!"*

Enoch stared dumbfounded at the telephone and then jabbed at the *"4"* button. Enoch listened to the sound of loud punk music – *God Save the Queen!* – Together with laughter and shouting of a house party. After thirty seconds, a squeaky cockney voice of a drunken punkette demanded *"OK, let's hear your success story, love!"* The exasperated Enoch whimpered *"Excuse me, is this Sperm Mart customer services?"* The woman giggled and replied *"Yeah, suppose you could call it that! Can you make it snappy darlin', because this is a great party?"*

Enoch explained that he made an order the previous evening. *"Yeah, darling, that's our charmer, Joe. He said your missus had a great time!"* *"But..,"* stammered Enoch, *"We cannot find the IC Toolkit we ordered."* The assistant replied that *"the job"* had been fulfilled, and Lucy had given Joe the maximum feedback rating for service. You will have a baby in nine months time! Take care, darling! Bye!" The telephone conversation and accompanying sound of The Sex Pistols terminated abruptly, and the bemused Enoch was greeted by the purring sound of a disconnected phone line.

Afterwards Enoch did his utmost to erase the memory of the *"extraterrestrial intrusion."* He deemed the event to be a dream and they entered into an unspoken contract to deny it, and to avoid mentioning the event, if possible.

Within twelve weeks of the *"event"*, Lucy's abdomen had swollen and she knew she was hosting a living being. Lucy tried to conceal her pregnancy from Enoch, so she wore baggy woolen jumpers and other loose-fitting clothes. Sometimes she would sob uncontrollably and binge upon several packets of brandy snap biscuits and chocolate mousse. In the evenings, she would sit in the sun lounge and gaze into the sky, mesmerized by the glitter of enchanting stars.

Enoch was temporarily incapacitated by *"some foreign bacterial invasion."* His physical condition deteriorated the moment he heard that his friendly neighbors, Teddy and Lacrosse, would be replaced by a black unemployed football player and his fashion model wife.

On the following Sunday afternoon, Enoch and Lucy visited Enoch's parents for tea and cream cakes. The appointment was essentially a duty to show respect for their parents. Enoch and Lucy dressed in smart clean clothes for the occasion. Boy added sheen to the car by washing it clean, waxing the enamel and carefully buffing it for the occasion.

Enoch's mother had the brittle appearance of a porcelain doll, a bird's nest of cotton wool hair and bright red cheeks. The dainty mother's shrill voice was constantly fussing and gossiping. Furthermore, she always contained a smiling composure of gaiety.

Enoch's father was a bespectacled intellectual man with thinning salt 'n' pepper hair and a characteristic birthmark - the size of a crown coin - above his left cheek. He had a passion for classical music, literature and fine art.

He constantly recanted famous quotations and quirky anecdotes.

Enoch and Lucy were ushered into the dining room where they were seated around an antique table which was covered with a lace cloth embroidered with violets. The table hosted fine crockery, silver cutlery, a china teapot, white napkins inside ivory holders, butter tray, a pot of homemade strawberry jam and a large sponge cake bulging with whipped cream and peaches.

After Enoch's father recited grace, he launched into a monologue about national politics and the winners and losers of the stock market. The sentences were punctuated by Enoch's compliant nods of agreement and such exclamations as *"Absolutely!"*, *"Yes!"* and *"Rather!"*

Enoch's mother suddenly focused her attention on Lucy's midriff and exclaimed *"Lucy, dear, do you have some special news for us?"* Lucy and Enoch stared at each other aghast in sheer horror. Lucy whispered *"Yes, I think so."* The father announced *"A celebration is in order!"* as he opened the drinks cabinet and picked out four sherry glasses and a bottle of Martini.

"Your creative spirit shall be rewarded!" said Enoch's father as he handed sealed envelopes to the couple. *"And let's buy the Mercedes for you next week!"* he said. *"Oh. It's just delightful news… oh how happy I am for you both! At last, we will be grandparents,"* said Enoch's mother in her shrill voice.

During the following six months, Lucy experienced intermittent fits of depression and euphoria; and during these periods she would binge on marsh mallows and puff away on cigarettes. Eventually Lucy began to experience contractions. Enoch instructed Boy to drive her to the local maternity hospital because he had an important meeting *"about the problem of the noisy neighbors."*

Lucy lay on the bed in the maternity ward screaming to the beat of each contraction. Lucy was surrounded by the Head Midwife, her assistant and the resident doctor. The doctor advised the midwife, *"The contractions are not strong enough. Let's use the suction cap to assist this delivery."*

The Head Midwife checked the fetal monitor and reported critically low heart rate of the baby. *"The baby has fetal distress so we need delivery pronto!"* The midwife attached the suction cap on the baby's crown and the device was switched on.

The suction level was increased to the highest setting, and still the baby would not dislodge from the comfort of Lucy's womb. *"Push harder!"* screamed the midwife. *"This baby is so stubborn!"* exclaimed the doctor. Suddenly there was a great electric flash and all the electric appliances failed. *"It's a power failure. The backup generators should switch on automatically, but they are not."*

Then the three alien punks walked into the ward. *"Who do you think you are?"* asked the doctor. *"We are the three wise aliens. And who the f**k are you?"* Joe didn't wait for the doctor's response; he walked straight over to Lucy. He performed a bizarre shamanic ritual and within seconds he was holding a newborn baby.

Joe handed the baby to the midwife. *"Voila! The autographs come later!"* he said. The midwife immediately clamped the umbilical chord and suctioned the baby's nose. While the baby wailed, the midwife removed the placenta and checked the condition of Lucy's uterus.

Lucy slept at the hospital that evening. The following morning Boy arrived to collect her and drive them back home. Enoch greeted them in the front garden. He opened the passenger door and hesitantly surveyed the shrouded baby. The baby instantly started wailing. *"Oh, darling, the smell is just revolting!"* Enoch retreated to the azaleas in the back garden.

The perplexed Enoch stared at the orange petals of the azalea and pleadingly asked it, *"What on Earth are we going to do?"* Then gradually his face transformed into a serene expression as he was struck by the lightning bolt of inspiration. *"Thanks, petal!"* he said as he walked towards the house. Enoch was a man with a mission.

Enoch was keen to deliver his news to his old school buddies at The Wheat Sheaf public house. *"If we have to endure such repugnant odors and offensive wails, we must at least allow ourselves some respite!"* announced Enoch before leaving.

The usual crowd was there: Eric the stock broker wearing plus fours; Teddy, clutching his walking stick as usual; Barry the property developer, and Rupert who breeds labradors. Enoch bought a round of bitter ales after announcing his recent fatherhood.

Enoch's drinking chums are especially jocular on such occasions, and Rupert the dog breeder had a penchant for infantile toasts. *"Let's make a toast for soiled nappies!"* he declared, holding his glass towards Enoch. Enoch countered the gesture with the proverb, *"Children should be seen and not heard."* The clique erupted with laughter.

Enoch recounted the story about the electricity failure at the hospital. *"There was no electricity for ten minutes,"* he explained. *"What a sad start – and a dim start to a young man's life."* Enoch said. *"I know, we should call the little blighter, Sadim!"* Teddy was most impressed with the name.

After a few glasses of the local brew, Enoch revealed his plan of converting the baby's bedroom into a noise and smell-free sanitation zone. He explained that he would fill in the windows with bricks, and insulate the walls and ceilings with special foam designed to absorb noise pollution.

Teddy introduced the idea of installing a second door at the entrance to the room, to avoid *"lingering odors"*. *"Anyone leaving the room should pass through a decontamination zone where they shower and disinfect us against those disgusting germs. And the floor needs an integrated drainage system to expel the evil bodily secretions. Plus we must install powerful extractor fans to purify the air!"*

Enoch said, looking extremely pleased with his contribution. *"Gentlemen, I believe that between our masterminds, we have conceived the ultimate sight, sound and smell-proofed contamination chamber in history!"* A toast was made and many cheers followed.

"And, of course, we will have to rig up a catheter of Nestle milk for the blighter, so poor old Lucy doesn't have to get wailed at...," Enoch bragged in his alcoholic stupor. *"Of course, she should stick to the knitting!"* suggested Teddy guffawing.

Enoch instructed Bert Adams, the local builder, to convert Sadim's room into a pollution-contained sanitation zone. The project was completed within fifteen long sleepless days. The immaculate conversion, which was supported by high technology, delighted Enoch.

On the day the project was completed, Enoch invited old Teddy around for tea and a demonstration of the system. *"What a splendid job you have done, Enoch!"* he said as he stared at the control panel and CCTV monitor. *"How technology protects us from the vagaries of life!"* retorted Enoch smugly.

The television monitor revealed a monotone room of brilliant white, containing a cradle in the centre of the room. The original window had been filled with breeze blocks and a powerful extractor fan. Two surveillance cameras constantly roamed the space.

Enoch entertained teddy with a brief demo of the controls. *"Here are the temperature and pressure gauges,"* he said pointing to LCD screens. *"And this reading here shows us how much Nestle milk is left in the catheter."* Enoch explained that the system had sufficient capacity to feed the baby for two weeks without human intervention – *that's long enough for a skiing trip in France!"* Teddy was impressed, *"Jolly good stuff, Enoch."*

"Here is the volume dial, just in case you want to be reminded of the sound of a wailing baby." Enoch carefully rotated the dial clockwise, so the sound of Sadim's screaming was audible. *"I think that's enough, Teddy!"* said Enoch, clicking the volume dial back to zero.

Enoch explained to Teddy about his sound and odor-proof insulation membrane. It is a patented synthetic rubber membrane which contains special components to absorb the menacing sounds and pungent odors of screaming babies… and by Jove, it's effective… *last night I slept like a log … I did not hear a squeak from the little blighter!"*

"Oh, yes, there's just one bone of contention – we still have to change nappies three times a day, but I found a solution for that problem too. Young Boy, the gardener, volunteered to get truly soiled..ha ha!! I suppose I ought to give the young lad a bonus," Enoch surmised.

Teddy and Enoch retired to the sun lounge with a pot of Earl Grey tea, where they agreed that all of life's challenges can be overcome by applying organizational skills intelligently. *"And let's face it, common sense is not too common nowadays - in an age when niggers are overthrowing our empire… God help us, Teddy!"*

CHAPTER 7

TRICKSTERS IN LOVE & LUST

THE KAMMU ORPHAN

The Kammu hill tribe settled across northern Laos, Vietnam, Thailand and Southern China. The Kammu people are treated as inferior people in most parts of Indochina. In Kammu folk tales the orphan is a symbol for an oppressed victim; whereas the governor represents the oppressor. A story about a Kammu orphan follows:

A poor Kammu orphan worked in his rice field alone. He was never able to complete the task of harvesting the rice because the crop grew so quickly and he didn't have money to pay laborers to help him.

The governor of the village had seven wives who watched the orphan toil all day and they ridiculed him. *"You are so lazy and stupid! The rice grows faster than you can cut it, yet you only have one field!"* they said.

The orphan pointed to his basket which was overflowing with rice. *"See!"* said the orphan, *"I work from dawn to dusk each day, and there is always more work to be done."* But the seven women laughed at him and said, *"You're not a real man! You are unable to complete your duties as a man."*

The orphan reflected upon their words and said, *"Well, if all seven of you harvest my rice field, I will collect twenty loads of banana leaves for you. If you complete the job today, then I will be your servant boy. However, if you fail to*

finish the work today, I will take each of you as my wives."
The seven women agreed to the orphan's challenge.

The women toiled in the rice field all day, yet the rice grew faster than they could harvest it. Meanwhile, the orphan collected twenty basketfuls of banana leaves for them. By dusk the orphan observed that the women were unable to win the challenge.

The orphan walked to the Governor's residence and told him the story. Then the Governor asked his seven wives whether the story was true and they admitted it. *"Very well,"* said the Governor, *"then all seven of you will marry the orphan. Go, and leave me alone!"*

So the seven women married the orphan and they all lived together. However none of them allowed him to have sex with them. They slept in the same room together, but they refused to let him touch them.

One day the orphan caught a monkey in his trap. Although the monkey was dead, its penis was still erect. He brought the dead animal back to his home and his wives asked, *"How did the monkey die?"*

The orphan told his wives that the monkey had f**ked himself to death. *"The monkey died from having too many females!"* The seven wives contemplated a while in silence until each of them smiled at each other triumphantly. *"If that's what happens when a man has too much sex, we must all f**k him to death, so we won't have to see him anymore!"*

That evening all seven women had sex with the orphan and each of them begat babies. Instead of dying of exhaus-

178

tion, the orphan enjoyed his marital life. The Governor, on the other hand, became lonely. In later years the orphan's children tended to the rice fields and they all lived happily ever after.

TRICKSTERS OF THE NIGHT

Katoey (or ladyboys) are the cheeky tricksters of the night who create the illusion of the female gender. In fact katoeys are men equipped with standard male gear.

The following excerpt from *Love Entrepreneurs* demarcates between katoey, transvestites, transsexuals and cross-dressers:

Katoey is a catch-all phrase referring to transvestites, transsexuals, over-the-top gays and cross-dressers. Cross-dressers are men who dress up in women's clothing because it makes them feel sexy.

Transvestites are men who dress up as women more convincingly, and that's who you will see at most of the cabarets in Thailand. Transvestites are not transsexuals, but straight men who look like women for the duration of the show.

Transsexuals are men who are making the transition to becoming women and they use either chemicals or surgery to accomplish it. The pre-operative (*"pre-op"*) transsexual may have had breast augmentation and probably is taking hormone shots (estrogen shots), which tend to inhibit hair growth and add a padding of baby fat on the elbows and take away the sharp edges associated with masculinity. Post-op transsexuals go the full distance with a sex-change operation. This is called Sex Re-Assignment Surgery (SRS).

Most of the katoey in Thailand are pre-op. They do not take the final step because the operation is irreversible and there is a great risk of losing the ability to have orgasm. Most katoey want to keep their dicks! And, according to Jerry Hopkins, *"A lot of men want a woman with breasts and a penis."*

Katoey are part of the underground vampire culture, for they sleep during the daytime and live for the night time. They are highly-sexed predators, adept in the art of seduction, who attach to their prey and suck them dry.

Naturally katoey are world class actors or drama queens. They are not women, yet they appear more feminine than women. Katoey love to exaggerate the wiggle of their hips and captivate their audience with their smile and cheeky demeanor. When they hook their customers, they reel them in, and they bleed them just like Count Dracula.

Stories abound of foreigners taken for a ride by stunning ladies (with penises). Sometimes they drug their customers before cavorting with them and running away with their wallets. Katoey are the funniest tricksters of the night with an impressive portfolio of con tricks up their sleeves.

Count Dracula's sexual predators seldom see the light of day so they are pale skinned and Goth-like. Many katoey imbibe amphetamines to maintain their frenzy while ordinary people are slumbering. Yanisa, a ladyboy from Chonuri, says health insurers consider their occupation high risk and will not touch them.

For further exploration of the world of katoey check out *Gender Illusionists* (with Jerry Hopkins) in *Love Entrepreneurs* by Phil Nicks.

TAX MAXIMIZATION CONSULTING

The following contemporary trickster story which is in two parts was written by business broker, Phil A. Stein, in Thailand.

<u>PART I</u>

It's 9.30am and I am sitting at my desk, armed with my cup of sickly-tasting 3-in-1 coffee. (I must remember to get a proper coffee machine sometime). I am waiting for the day to begin.

Suddenly the phone rings. Nui, our secretary, hands me the telephone. *"It's a Thai lady called Mook. She wants to know how she can pay tax."* My day has begun.

"Good morning, Khun Mook. My name is Phil. I am the manager of Big Belt Consulting. How can I help you?"

"I want to know how I can pay tax," she says. *"Did you say you want to find out how you can pay tax?"* I asked, surprised and confused. *"Good!"* I say, wondering whether the person on the other end of the line is a lunatic. Then I arranged a meeting with her.

As the myriad tax rules and regulations get more complex, the task of finding a suitable path through the fiscal jungle becomes extremely complicated. This has lead to the emergence of tax consultancy, one of the most mentally challenging and lucrative professions. As a general rule, working class *"proletariat"* willingly pay their taxes, rich people avoid taxes (whilst complying with the law of the land), and the rest evade taxes. This morning is an exception to the rule.

"Good afternoon, Khun Mook!" Mook, arrives - with her girlfriend in tow - on time, which is unusual in Chiang Mai. They are both young – mid twenties - small, attractive, chirpy little birds.

Mook explains that her American boyfriend is sending her five hundred US dollars each month and that she wants to go travelling abroad. I told her, I wish I had friends like hers. She giggled. Then she explains her problem that she is unable to substantiate her income for the Embassy. So she needs to establish a legitimate income. The officials at the Embassy asked her to prove her income by showing receipts of personal tax paid.

We discuss alternative solutions to her problem. Mook liked the idea of being a Managing Director of her own limited company.
"What service would your company provide?" I ask.
"Website marketing services," she replies.
"Really?" I am very interested. *"Are you good at internet marketing?"* I ask.
"No, not really," she says, smiling.
That's no problem, I think, as long as she is not asking us to launder entertainment industry income.

Stories abound of young Thai ladies who have many foreign *"boyfriends"*, each sending them monthly stipends from overseas. Some receive as many as twenty monthly deposits (of around five hundred US Dollars). Ten thousand dollars per month goes a long way in Thailand.

I am pleased that I can enable these young women to travel internationally. I feel extremely lucky to have had the opportunity to travel so much in my life. It's a great education. Now I am helping these cheeky girls to break down international borders. Our consultancy assists these chirpy little birds spread their wings and fly away from their nest! It's called Liberation Management.

PART II

I placed a job advertisement in a local newspaper for a part-time website marketing assistant. A Thai lady called Jenni submitted her curriculum vitae which was full of gaping holes. She obviously had an enterprising bent - perfect for the job!

I met Jenni in Starbucks. She arrived in black attire. Her arm was grazed, presumably the result of a motorcycle accident. And she had that *"customer services"* smile.

Jenni explained to me that 99% of the internet is sex-related. Well, I thought, I have been absorbed with the remaining 1%. After more conversation, I could not buy her story. This woman was from the entertainment industry, yet she presented herself as an SEO (Search Engine Optimization) specialist.

I wrote a brief email to Jenni asking her to respect confidentiality and to be transparent about any foreign partner she might have. Naturally I want to know the person who is really working with me.

This is the response I received via email:

Hi Khun Alex,

Let me explain how this business works.

I am doing SEO for you on a freelance basis. I will not discuss the work I do with you with my other clients, but you have no say in my other business. Please do not jump to conclusions or assume that I am going to be sharing your secrets with other people: I won't, because I have no interest in doing this. Because I am a freelance, I will by definition have other clients, because I'm good at what I do.

No matter where you look, you will not find other terms. The alternative to this is to hire someone to work for you full time and pay them a good salary. For SEO work, this would be at least 20,000 baht per month.

I will keep the details of my work for you confidential. However, I am doing SEO for you. SEO (search engine optimization) is done to allow your business to be found more easily by your potential customers. There must, by definition, be some details about your business which are shared: otherwise, nobody will find your business.

There is no way that you are a credible MI6, CIA or KGB agent. The extreme measures you are taking to protect your password are unnecessary: I have no interest in sharing it with anyone, and nobody knows about your business yet, and so nobody has any interest in stealing your password.

If I work for you, I promise you will be happy with the results. However, I have no time for games.

Regards, Jenni

Well, does that seem like an email from a Thai lady? Of course not! The email was actually written by a 35 year old American, using Jenni as a front for his SEO business.

MR PINK'S SECRET

I am sitting at the bar called *The Reservoir Dogs*, chatting to Mr Pink, one of the bar's owners. The long rectangular room is noticeably angular and dark; the natural habitat for the ever-edgy Mr Pink. The ceiling and walls are painted black, matching the colour of his heart. My friend, Mr Violet, suggests the absence of curvature in this drinking den – including females - might trigger an anxiety attack in any tender-hearted feng shui expert.

Mr Pink

Mr Pink is a bulky man with silky white skin underneath his armour of scary tattoos, mainly monsters, demons and reptilian skulls. He sports a large paunch – comparable to a damsel's belly after 7 month's gestation (or three months for an elephant) – essentially a bi-product of countless hours of work - drinking *Tigress* beer - and he admits to being a workaholic. Mr Pink wears the standard rebel outfit: black baseball cap, back-to-front – geezer-style - under his short-cropped hair. His t-shirt emblazons the word Joker above a caricature of an idiot.

Women are not strictly banned from The Dogs' bar but their entry is not encouraged. Stray woman occasionally visit this macho hideout but they are ignored. The bar's patrons use the den as a refuge from women; to lament their pair-shaped relationships, past or present. One day God played an ironic joke on Mr Pink by sending a clique of local deaf mute women to the bar who claimed it as their new living room.

At the rear of The Dogs' bar there is a sofa and two armchairs surrounding a coffee table. This cavernous

187

space is the home of the deaf mute girls. Two of the customers learnt to communicate with the girls in sign language. *"It's so much easier than the Thai language"* admits Mr Maroon. Mr Pink resents the presence of the deaf mutes so his partner reminds him that they bring trade to his bar.

Miss Pink (#1)

Mr Pink is lamenting the behaviour of Miss Pink, his ex-girlfriend. She stole his motorbike and his gold jewellery. Miss Pink is a sassy woman and an exhibitionist too. She gives her audience the impression she needs more tender loving care than she receives. She always places herself at the epicentre of her G-spotted chaotic Universe.

Miss Pink talks loud 'n' dirty about various parts of her anatomy and she enjoys describing her faecal matter too. Mr Pink explains she is schizophrenic and emotionally unstable; whereas Mr Indigo, Mr Pink's business partner, curtly sums her up as *"a total nutter."* Miss Pink has been the primary catalyst for many explosive dramas during the enfoldment of The Reservoir Dog's history.

Mr & Miss Pink's *"relationship"* eventually imploded, leaving a graveyard of shattered glass in the aftermath of the meltdown. During this chaos Miss Pink was meeting Mr Crimson, a local guest house proprietor. When Mr Pink heard about Mr Crimson's surreptitious meetings with *"his woman,"* he smashed myriad glasses in an alcohol-fuelled frenzy and exercised his authority; he banned Mr Crimson from his bar. This was an ill-conceived strategy because Mr Crimson was one of the bar's best spenders; he even settled his bar tabs, unlike many of the other patrons. Afterwards Mr Crimson took Miss Pink and company to other local drinking establishments.

Miss Pink #2 (#2)

After a few weeks of hard work (in various karaoke bars) Mr Pink met Miss Pink #2 (aka: #2). Meanwhile #1 raced off to oblivion on Mr Pink's motorbike with his money. #2 brings new hope to Mr Pink in the domain of relationship dynamics.

Miss Pink #2 is elegant, and has a rather posh American accent. She claims to be a member of Thailand's *"High So'"* (high society). #2 was educated in USA. Many of the bar's patrons – including Mr Pink - believed #2 is real *"class"*. During Mr Pink's courting ritual with Chiang Mai's debutante, he agreed to forego sex for the first month or so; a small price to pay for proper class in the bedroom. Then one day this illusion was shattered...

Mr Brown visited the bar one evening and noticed #2. When he heard her voice he immediately recognised her. Mr Brown explained to me that #2 was his first girlfriend in Chiang Mai! He divulged that she had a serious substance-abuse issue, causing her to steal a large wedge of cash from his wallet. A week later I met another customer who explained that #2 took numerous "boyfriends" to a jewellery shop in Chiang Mai's infamous red light area. Miss Pink #2's sheen tarnished overnight. After a few weeks her voice was seldom heard.

Miss Pink #3 (#3)

Mr Pink packs a wedge of Snus next to his gum, underneath his top lip. He tells me about his new lady friend,

Miss Pink #3, who he discovered at a local karaoke bar. Mr Pink boasts that she gives him Chiang Mai's best blowjob every morning. Apparently her cooking is good too. Mr Pink is quite the tough man. He enhances his macho image by socialising exclusively with other tough guys with equally scary tattoos. I notice he has a hair-lip scar which enhances the perception of crowbar-wielding abilities.

The ever-friendly guest house proprietor, Mr Crimson, struts into Mr Pink's world yet again. This time Mr Crimson lures #2 away from the darkest of the Dogs' shadows. When Mr Pink discovered this further act of treachery, his ensuing tantrums caused many glass missiles to fragment on both sides of the bar.

Mr Pink's Secret

Later that evening a young Thai guy sits next to Mr Pink at the bar. His name is Mr Blue. They are engaged in conversation while I drink and observe. They are laughing a lot. Mr Pink seems to be sensually aroused as he gyrates his pelvis in the rotating barstool. Mr Blue is responding in a similar way. Although there is no direct physical contact between the two men, they are engaged in a powerfully intimate sensual dance. How can I recognise this? Maybe I was bisexual in a previous life? However, my observation of their body language leaves me in no doubt that Mr Pink is either gay or bi-sexual. I am in awe of this hilarious revelation, almost exploding with amusement.

Three weeks later our friend, Mr Green, arrives in Chiang Mai from Greenland. A group of friends from the bar organised a trip to the dam at Maetang in his honour. However Mr Green declined this invitation, preferring to go on an alternative trip with Mr Pink and Mr Black. When they returned, Mr Green recounted his tale of alcoholic bingeing. He was clearly unstable after excessive drinking marathons.

Mr Green explained that he discovered something but he was unable to tell me what. After a beer or two, Mr Green told me anyway. Mr Green said Mr Pink admitted that he was gay! Later Mr Green tried to backtrack on this assertion, saying he was in an alcohol-induced dream-state so Mr Pink's confession may have been illusory! Mr Green was clearly very worried that Mr Pink would discover Mr Green's breach of confidentiality.

The following morning, Mr Green visits my room looking traumatised, beads of perspiration running down his forehead. What's up? I ask Mr Green. Mr Green explains that he had experienced a nightmare. In his dream, Mr Pink discovered that Mr Green had divulged Mr Pink's secret. Mr Pink, in his anger, grabbed a mallet and chased Mr Green. Eventually Mr Pink caught up with Mr Green and whacked the metal tool on Mr Green's forehead. Mr Green screamed with pain, spontaneously waking up. He got out of bed and walked into the bathroom mirror. He noticed blood on his forehead. Immediately he realised that a mosquito had bitten him and maybe he had scratched the resulting lump.

Mr Green confirmed my belief about Mr Pink's sexuality. I do not judge people by their culture, sexual preference, age, religion or choice of underwear; but, alas, I am a human being! I don't care whether Mr Pink wears ladies underwear or not, but he can't accept his sexuality. I wonder whether he will ever venture outside of his closet?

Who cares whether the bar owner of The Reservoir Dogs is gay, kinky or heterosexual as long as they are being honest? However, according to his dress code, Mr Pink is a joker.

Mr Green's Demon Tattoo

Mr Green is back in town to drink the bar dry again! This time Mr Pink persuades Mr Green to part with a massive THB30,000 on the ugliest *"demon"* tattoo in town. However, Mr Green reckons he was given not only a bargain, but a discount of 20%! According to other customers, Mr Pink paid between two and three times the standard price for such work (in Manchester)!

I asked Mr Green who supplied his body graffiti. He told me the *"artist"* is called Mr Ugly. Later I commented to Mr Pink about how Mr Green had been properly fleeced. Mr Pink's mood changed instantly; he became morose and retired to the darts board without saying anything.

Since Mr Pink referred Mr Green to Mr Ugly, under Thai custom he would be eligible to an introduction fee (of say 20%). If I received introduction fees for the customers I had introduced to the bar – including Mr Green, Mr Violet and Mr & Ms White – I would be a rich man, indeed.

Anyway, Mr Green is a generous man. He gave an expensive mobile phone to one of the deaf mutes as a *"leaving present"*. Perhaps a megaphone would be as useful, but it's the thought which counts. However, the woman did use the text-messaging function to request more money from Mr Green, while he was busily saving money in Greenland for his next assault on his liver.

The Ice Pick

One evening I was sitting at Somphet Market eating some Japanese food, when Miss Pink #3 appeared and sat down next to me. She explained that she was not happy with Mr Pink and she would *"test him to see whether he really loved her"*. At the time I had no idea what she was talking about; I just thought *"now I am talking to yet another insane Thai lady!"*

Four weeks later I am sitting at the bar when Mr Black rushes in proclaiming that #3 has just stabbed Mr Pink in the belly with an ice pick. Then Mr and Mrs Black set off to Chiangmai Ram hospital to see whether Mr Pink is still alive. Later we found out that Mr Pink had actually been stabbed with a knife; he was recovering.

A few weeks after this drama #3 said she is still very much in love with Mr Pink. Some Thai women have strange ways of expressing their affections.

Two weeks later, at Mr and Ms White's wedding party, and after a couple of bottles of Thai whisky, Mr Pink announces he is a daddy-to be. Alas, #3 is pregnant! This was one of those occasions when I was totally gob-smacked. The booze was beginning to *"kick in"* as the punk band, Bangkok Alcohol, screamed *"We Don't Care!"*

After another bottle of *100 Pipers* whisky, Mr Pink tells us #3 insists on keeping the baby. She wants to keep Mr Pink too. Unfortunately Mr Pink wants neither #3 nor the baby. Mr Pink's hairlip scar seems to be glowing as he stares menacingly into his empty whisky glass.

Chiang Mai's ultimate Concept Bar

During Mr & Ms White's wedding party, Mr Pink divulges his ingenious counter-strategy. This plan is so clever, it left me dumb-founded. Here it is: Mr Pink will snatch the baby away from #3 while she is off-guard (when she is applying eye-liner in ladies' room perhaps). Then he will take the baby away *"in hiding"* and bring the baby up himself.

I wonder how Mr Pink would manage to raise a baby on his own, in between binge-drinking and clandestine internet trading. I imagine a carrycot underneath the darts board with various fluffy toys, milk feeding-bottle (with rubber teat) and bibs scattered around the bar. After a few months, Mr Pink might install a *"baby bouncer"* next to the optics.

"The Dogs" could conceivably become Chiang Mai's ultimate concept bar: the only bar in town with a crèche. Imagine drunken farang singing baby lullabies, competing with heavy metal band, Metallica. I wonder whether the barman's duties would include nappy-changing and bottle-feeding from a Sang Som bottle.

Mr Crimson Returns

Alas, these ideas are mere idle speculation! However, it is known that Mr Crimson was in town during the previous four months. Mr Crimson, who has already established a sound track record for pursing Mr Pink's lady friends, obviously shares his taste in women. Recently Mr Brown was the acolyte and bearer of a sinister revelation: he saw #3 eating noodles with Mr Crimson at Somphet market.

The mind is a remarkable tool and it may be used to generate millions of ideas and calculations consecutively. In this case, my mind produced a *"What If?"* scenario. Here it is: What if Mr Pink snatches the baby away from #3, and brings s/him up alone, later to discover Mr Crimson is the real father? Surely Mr Crimson would be the champion joker, unless Mr Pink consciously plays cruel jokes on himself?

Mr Crimson would cockily adulate Mr Pink for kindly offering years of tender motherly care to his son. The son's tearful reunion with his father would enrage the gender-confused Mr Pink, causing yet another volley of glass missiles in Mr Crimson's direction.

I share these grave speculations with Mr Green over a beer at The Dogs. We settle our bills and, as usual, Mr Green leaves a large tip for the barman. I mention that tips at The Dogs' bar are pooled and shared between each of the business partners. So when we buy a drink for the barman, the profit component – about half the price - is split between the shareholders. Mr Yellow says he only gives tips to people who offer a *"value-added service"* (not VAT). After all, nuclear scientists and swimming pool attendants never receive tips. Do you? He asks. Anyway, does receiving a blowjob count as a *"value-added service?"* muses Mr Yellow.

Mr Beige is Saved

After Mr and Mrs Whites' wedding party, Mr Red kindly gives me a cd of photographs of the event. I think of ways to reciprocate and decide to send him this story about the Reservoir Dogs' Bar via email.

Several weeks later I meet Mr Pink's business partner who plays in a jazz band. After watching the performance we both enjoy a drink together. After a beer he says *"I have a bone to pick with you"*. Here we go again. *"What's the problem?"* I ask cheerily, feeling a lead ingot pushing down on my stomach. Since everyone knows about Mr Pink's Secret, none of the regulars visit the bar any longer. Even Mr Pink doesn't visit the bar any longer.

Later I meet Mr Beige. He explains that he has quit alcohol and smoking. He has turned a new leaf in the annals of The Reservoir Dogs'. Later he was seen with Mr Crimson, shaking hands with a reverend at a local Bible College.

SURVEILLANCE TECHNOLOGY

If you detect a single lie, you have identified the "tip of the iceberg", so change course immediately or you will go down like the Titanic.
- Phil Nicks with Warren Olsen

This chapter is all about checking out the suitability of your partner-to-be. Relationship commitments have many serious implications which can affect your health, wealth, social and legal status. A few simple background checks and pertinent questions will help you to avoid the common pitfalls.

Love auditing, family background checking, investigation into suspected cases of infidelity and the task of shedding light on *"the truth, the whole truth and nothing but the whole truth"* offers myriad profitable opportunities to Love Entrepreneurs. There are some simple techniques described in this chapter which can reduce relationship *"risk"* and potentially save you thousands of dollars and untold suffering.

The famous Bangkok private investigator, Warren Olsen, who wrote the book *Confessions of a Bangkok Private Eye* with Stephen Leather, offers his insights about how to really understand Asian people.

As with all relationships, the key to harmony is trust. If you cannot trust your partner your intuition is probably not deceiving you. As warren Olsen says, you just need to detect one lie. A person who lies once lies a million times. And it's not too difficult to detect just one lie.

Background Checks

What follows is a list of straightforward tests to validate your partner-to-be.

Control questions are an effective way of detecting lies. A control question is a question which can easily be checked. For example, the answer to *"How old are you?"* can easily be verified against the subject's identity card (butprachachun). Checking the ID card is a good place to start because it confirms the person's sexual identity in lands of smiling lady-boys.

Control events are effective ways of calibrating a person's honesty. For example, leave a seemingly mislaid banknote or two somewhere around your home. Then wait and see whether your partner *"fetches"* it and returns the property to its rightful owner like an obedient golden re-triever.

Employment

Find out your partner's employer, and phone her at work. To validate her employer it is necessary to make a direct phone call to her while she is at her employer's address. Leaving a phone message and subsequent call back does not count because she could be phoning back from a different location.

Unaccounted Husbands and Children

It is not always easy to check whether your Thai lady has a husband or children because there is no centralized marriage registry. Marriages are usually registered at either party's local amphur office. However, some marriages, like common law relationships, are sealed socially by village ceremony and the transfer of gold without formal registration. And some couples choose to register their marriage at a completely different amphur office, and there are hundreds of them in Thailand.

Thai people are meant to register their home at the local amphur office. They should be listed on the property document *(tabienbaan)* for their residential address. This property book lists all the registered Thai citizens living at the property. Of course the document should list any children living at the address.

Some Thai people do not reregister with their new local amphur office when they move address. This makes it extremely difficult to confirm their residential address.

Residential Address

Meet your partner-to-be at her real home address, whether it is registered or not. You have genuine cause for concern if she tries to stop you meeting her at her home unless she lives with her parents.

HIV Tests

Most Asians will agree to take a medical examination to check for sexually transmitted diseases, including HIV. But you should take the tests as well.

WARNING SIGNS

Eye Contact

A *"good"* Thai lady would never stare directly into a stranger's eyes while smiling at them. Such behavior is considered impolite. So if he or she does not return your direct eye contact, it may be a positive sign. But they may not like you anyway!

Many bargirls walking around the streets with their foreign customers flirt in this way with strangers.

Alcohol, Cigarettes & Drugs

In the Land of Smiles, many people indulge in pleasures to excess. Moderation is rare. So if you are attracted to someone who drinks alcohol or smokes, be wary. In Thai culture, decent ladies do not drink alcohol or smoke cigarettes. Their risk rating increases exponentially if she also flaunts a tattoo on her body.

Foreign Targets

Freelance predators target foreign men who have not stayed in Asia for more than a few weeks. They don't want to meet men who have stayed – or strayed – for too long. If they find out you are learning the local language, they will instantly vanish into the ethers. They want fresh innocence, gullibility and untapped coffers – ideally straight from the airport.

THE UNTOUCHABLES

According to Yanisa, who writes the *Love Rules* column for Guru Magazine, you should steer clear from the following women at all costs:

- Your friend's ex-girlfriend or sister
- Hairdressers
- Your PA or secretary
- The ex-girlfriend
- The hot professional you meet at a club or party
- A go-go girl
- High maintenance *"HiSo"* (high society) women

Perhaps Yanisa is a bit hard on hairdressers, but they do tend to have a penchant for gossiping; and they have relationship opportunities in abundance no matter how entrepreneurial they are.

Clearly it's wise to keep a wide birth from the blood-sucking predators who frequent trendy nightclubs and bars. Dating your best friend's sister or ex-girlfriend is the perfect formula for disaster; as is dating your personal assistant or secretary.

It's never a wise idea to date your best friend's sister whether you are in Chiang Mai or Cheltenham, Hua Hin or Huston. And getting serious with a go-go dancer is seriously demented behavior in any part of the world.

Don't date your clients, your students, family members, anyone underage or your colleagues at work. This simple principle should not be a problem because there are over 6 billion people in the world to choose from.

The list of untouchables should be extended to include:
- Anyone with alcoholics, gamblers or heavily-laden debtors in their family
- Ladies or gentlemen who will not to show you where they live

INTERVIEWING TECHNIQUES

Warren Olsen wrote a research paper for Victoria University in New Zealand, entitled *"Investigative Interviewing of Asians"* in conjunction with government agencies. Part of his research focuses on epistemology, the science of reasons for the way people think.

The interview should always begin with unarmed soft questions, particularly about friends and family. The interview will not be effective if you rush in with the direct *"killer questions"* which make them feel defensive.

It is beneficial to interview Asians in a restaurant where you can eat together. Warren comments *"much time is spent beating around the bush, until finally the birds fly out!"*

"Direct or armed questions are not generally the best approach. Asian people tend not to rush things. An indirect approach, working slowly around to your main questions will render better results. Spending time to get information about their home and family is a good way to start, and offering sustenance is also appreciated. Interrogation of Asians will normally take longer than an interview with a westerner." Warren Olsen

Warren recommends not using negative phraseology when questioning Asians:

Negative phraseology discourages interviewees and leads to *"I don't know"* answers. Eg: *"You don't know his name, do you?"* In this case, they may answer *"Yes"*, meaning *"Yes, I don't know"*, whereas a westerner would normally reply in the negative, meaning *"No, I don't know"*.

Be careful when your questions refer to the past or future because many Asians have no *"tense"* indicators in their language. This problem can be avoided by referring to specific dates or events. Eg *"What did you do on Labor Day in 2006?"*

According to Warren, allowing the Asian interviewee a way of saving face is an effective way of getting a confession. An example is: *"Did you take the money because you wanted to play cards with your friends, or did you feel under obligation to help your family?"* Cheating to help family is considered by many Asians as both responsible and honorable.

Direct sales professionals adopt a similar technique for closing deals; *The Wellington Close* pushes your target into a corner with words like *"Do you want to buy the red one or do you prefer it in black?"* A similarly manipulative psychological approach to extract favor from your romantic suitor is *"What is it you like so much about me? Is it my honesty or my blue eyes?"* The truth always flows easier during light-hearted banter.

Never raise your voice or admonish an Asian interviewee in public. They will *"shut down"* their communication if they lose face.

Be aware that many Asians will make up an answer rather than admitting that they don't know the answer. Not only do they want to avoid seeming ignorant to the questioner, they want to please the interviewer too. One expatriate in Southeast Asia commented: *"Asians care more about feelings than truth."*

Asian interpreters, referred to as "a necessary evil" in some detective agencies, often support interviewees in subtle ways; for example, by flexing the meaning of key words to favor their fellow Asian. Warren always positioned his interpreters behind his suspect, so they could not communicate with each other by eye contact, hand signals, nods or other non-verbal signals.

Todd's Biting Questions

There is a book entitled *"One Thousand Questions to Ask Your Lover-To-Be"* to help you assess the suitability of your partner-to-be. With so many anal questions like *"How many milligrams of Sodium Chloride do you have with your Penang curry?"* you will be extremely busy, stressed and probably paranoid. Perhaps a more appropriate title for that book would be Operation Mindfcuk.

Todd Hamilton has three succinct – yet biting – questions which cut through all the bull. Here they are:

Question # 1: What is your goal in life (or vision)?

Many Thai ladies have no goals or clear vision about their future. They are grounded in the present moment. A satisfactory answer to the question is *"To return to my parents' village to take care of my parents."* A diminishing number of Thais are prepared to make such a commitment to their family nowadays. If they have the goodwill to look after their parents through their declining years, you have a better chance of being looked after in old age yourself.

Question # 2: What is your financial situation?

Is he or she currently able to support herself and her family, and does she have any savings? If she is unable to support herself then she is probably needy – and that's not a good basis for a relationship because she probably needs your money more than she needs you! If she has some savings, this demonstrates financial savvy, and she can invest in a family home as a genuine partner.

Question # 3: What does your family need from me?

If the Thai lady's family is either insincere or greedy take the next exit. Find out whether there are any chronic alcoholics, gamblers or heavily debt-laden family members. Does the family expect a dowry *(Sin Sot)*, and if so, would they agree to return some or all of it after the wedding? It may be beneficial to meet the lady's parents long before discussing marriage to get the answer to this question.

HANDY GADGETS

Asian women, and especially Thai ladies, love to keep secrets to themselves. They are practical people and don't want to make themselves more vulnerable than necessary. But now computer technology enables their suspicious partners to discover their secrets at minimal cost.

It's quite surprising - and scary – knowing what surveillance technology is available. These software applications can be downloaded onto your computer within minutes for the cost of a round of drinks.

The most common items of surveillance technology are listed below. Neither the author nor the publisher necessarily advocates the use of such technology, unless absolutely necessary.

GPS

GPS enables users to track their chattels on computer-generated maps by inserting a small transmitter inside the target property. Vehicle hire companies use SPS technology to prevent theft of their stock of cars. If your partner has a tendency towards straying from home, you may want to plant a GPS-compatible transmitter in his or her vehicle or handbag. If you can't access his or her heart, at least you can access their territorial coordinates.

Here is a typical advertisement for GPS systems:

Super Bloodhound GPS Tracker is the essential hi-tech gadget for everyone wanting absolute order and control in their life. It is the prefect tool to record and view on 3D maps the whereabouts of your stray Thai lady or roaming farang man. All software is included. Confirm your doubts for only $269.00.

This powerful technology enables you to upload the geographical coordinates of your partner 24/7. You can implant the candid transmitters in almost any part of your partner's body, mobile phone, vehicle or bag. Easy!

Super Bloodhound GPS Tracker will help you develop trust in your relationship. Now you can buy real peace of mind for only $269.

GPS technology allows you to keep tabs on your spouse. The system also offers the potential for true love to blossom by enabling your spouse to actually demonstrate their fidelity. How can your love grow unless you are absolutely certain of their commitment to you?

Password Sniffers

If you sense that something in your relationship *"smells fishy"*, it's surely time to download a password sniffer onto your spouse's computer.

A password sniffer is a software application which enables detection of computer passwords typed into the computer device. Simply install a software program onto the computer used by your spouse or partner. The system will invisibly monitor all keystrokes on that computer and enable you to access the information remotely from your online account.

Password sniffers are useful in Thailand, where smell is taken seriously. Here, a person is judged according to their odor. So if a person has a pleasant smell – *hom* – he or she is considered a good person. Conversely the devil has a noxious – *men* – smell.

How can you possibly be taking your relationship seriously if you don't monitor every computer keystroke your spouse makes? You just need to make sure she isn't corresponding with other "boyfriends" around the globe. It is also helpful to monitor her bank account online to see how much her customers are sending her each month.

Password Sniffers enable you to:
- Capture every single keystroke they type, including passwords and usernames
- Read every email they receive or send
- View every webpage they visited and know how long they viewed it
- Monitor instant messages or online chat anytime
- Take screenshots of their computer screen at any time

Too many people invest hundreds of thousands of dollars in a legal relationship without properly monitoring its progress. It's like investing in a corporate stock and then not bothering to monitor the results of the company. Password sniffers enable your spouse to demonstrate their fidelity, allowing trust and true love to blossom.

Flexispy

As ex-Bangkok private eye, Warren Olsen, says *"the way to a Thai lady's heart is via her mobile phone."* Flexispy is the reason why.

Flexispy is a smart program which allows you to access your partner's SMS messages sent or received on their mobile phone. It is necessary to install a program on their mobile phone which must be compatible with the system. If their mobile phone is not compatible, simply give her a new mobile phone already loaded with Flexispy.

According to the Flexispy website which is aimed at suspicious men, the cheating wife's mobile phone is her Number 1 method of carrying on a affair. The system enables you to obtain a list of all phone contact numbers even after she has deleted them from her mobile.

Cheating wives commonly arrange last-minute liaisons or *"lunch meetings"* by sending an SMS, or making a phone call. An SMS that says *"need 2 c u so much"* is all you need, and Flexispy will find grab it for you.

Stray housewives frequently lie about their whereabouts, but with Flexispy *"location tracking"* you can verify her exact location anytime. Flexispy is totally dependable, and always truthful, unlike the adulterous spouse who pretends to be shopping in Central department store with her girlfriends.

Flexispy is a man's best friend. Whereas men favor technological control systems, women tend to prefer to use their superior instincts and communication skills to play the game. According to the Flexispy website,

> *"Women instinctively understand each gesture, smell and every subtle nuance of voice or facial expression and know what you are thinking. This enables her to throw you off her trail of her infidelity. She also has the ability to spot a hair on the bathroom floor and immediately identify whether it's her own or not."*

THE ART OF LYING

Polygraphs, usually known as lie detectors, are used by detectives and investigators to reveal mistruths.

According to Wikipedia, a polygraph is an instrument which measures and records physiological responses such as blood pressure, pulse, respiration and skin conductivity while the subject is interrogated. The polygraph measures physiological changes caused by the Sympathetic Nervous System during questioning. The FBI refers to polygraph-assisted interviews as a psychophysiological detection of deception (PDD) examination.

Some Asians are adept at lying though habit. In Asia there are infinite gradations grey in between the black and white lies. Some lies according to western culture are not considered lies in Asia. For example, cheating in order to support the family is usually considered honorable. Altering a story to save face is considered polite and responsible, so nobody feels hurt. So polygraphs are not as effective in Asia as in developed countries.

George W. Maschke and Gino J. Scalabrini, co-authors of *"The Lie behind the Lie Detector"*, do not believe the polygraphs. Perhaps they need to polygraph the lie detector? The authors claim that the technology is based upon deception rather than science. The following is an extract from their website:

"The person being "tested" is not supposed to know that while the polygraph operator declares that all questions must be answered truthfully, warning that the slightest hint of deception will be detected, he secretly assumes that denials in response to certain questions -- called "con-

trol" questions -- will be less than truthful. An example of a commonly used control question is, "Did you ever lie to get out of trouble?" The polygrapher steers the examinee into a denial by warning, for example, that anyone who would do so is the same kind of person who would commit the kind of behavior that is under investigation and then lie about it. But secretly, it is assumed that everyone has lied to get out of trouble."

Occasionally clients instruct introduction agencies to interview their selected candidates under polygraph. One such client was a 55 year old Filipino American control freak who was looking for a beautiful 20 year old Asian lady to marry. His plan was to finance her medical school training in America so she could nurse him properly throughout his old age.

There are several lie detectors available on the market. You can measure the length of your spouse's nose using a de-FIB-ulator. This hand-held gadget detects variations in a person's voice tension. The manufacturer claims the de-FIB-ulator is 65% accurate; perhaps not as accurate as intuition which comes free of charge.

One Polygraph Examination Agency offers to resolve your relationship if your spouse is straying. The company says they will not solve your issues but they will establish the truth (about the infidelity). Knowing the truth *"is a major hurdle in your reconciliation process, though we strongly suggest you seek the help of a qualified married counselor in addition to using the polygraph."* Another evangelical promise is: *"the truth will set you free."*

According to Warren Olsen, it is possible to cheat the polygraph by taking specific drugs. Liars enjoy cheating;

211

and one way of cheating is to bypass the means of detecting their lies. Liars don't need to take drugs to avoid detection by polygraph if they really believe their lies. The polygraph only works when the liar knows he or she is lying!

Perhaps the best people to spot liars are liars themselves, because liars think and behave the same way. Presumably this is why criminals make the best policemen.

GLOSSARY OF PUNK & TRICKSTER DEITIES

The following Gods are most influential to the punk movement. Most of the deities mentioned originate from Greek mythology.

We need Gods and heroes to inspire us to move onwards and upwards. Anyway, mythological tales are entertaining, and often reveal golden nuggets of wisdom.

Amun

Amun is the Egyptian God of elusiveness.

Asclepius

Apollo's son, Asclepius, was born on his mother's funeral pyre and fostered by the centaur, Chiron.

Asclepius's mother, Koronis, fell in love with a stranger while she was pregnant with Asclepius. When Apollo learnt of her disloyalty he killed her with an arrow. While Koronis lay on her funeral pyre, Apollo tore the baby Asclepius from her womb and asked Chiron to raise his son for him.

Chiron taught Asclepius to be an adept healer and a skilled physician. So the wounded healers, Chiron and his adopted son, both lost their parents at birth and became healers.

One day Asclepius was offered gold to revive a dead man and he accepted the assignment. Hades, God of the dead, complained to Zeus about the physician's breach of authority. Zeus struck Asclepius and his patient with his thunderbolt killing them both.

Ascepius's children also practiced as healers. His sons, Macaon and Podalirius, became surgeons; and his daughters were Hygeia, goddess of hygiene, and the elusive Panacea.

Bes

Bes is the Egyptian God of Music. Bes reincarnated as a member of the punk rock band, Happy Mondays, supplying mood enhancers to takers.

Chiron, The Wounded Healer

Chiron is the centaur known as *The Wounded Healer* from Greek mythology. Centaurs have the head, arms and chest of a human being, and the legs and abdomen of a horse. Centaurs embody untamed nature and have a reputation for unruly hedonism. They are indulgent drinkers and uncultured delinquents; just as punks are universally perceived.

Centaurs follow Dionysus, the God of nature, fertility, wine and spiritual intoxication. Therefore Dionysus is a great influence for punks, shamans and, indeed, The Punk Monk.

Chiron was the son of Cronus and Philyra, the nymph daughter of Oceanus. According to myth, Philyra transformed herself into a mare so she could escape from her suitor, Cronus. Undetered, Cronus changed himself into a horse so he could mate with her.

After copulating with Cronus, Philyra gave birth to the centaur, Chiron. She was so disgusted with herself for succumbing to sexual instinct, the ensuing reproduction caused her to turn herself into a tree. Thus, Chiron was abandoned by his parents; so Apollo - sun-god of music, poetry and the healing arts - became Chiron's foster father.

Myth states that Chiron wounded his knee when accidentally struck by Heracles' arrow[13]. Chiron's wound was so painful that he begged Zeus for the right to die and therefore relinquish his immortality. Zeus allowed Chiron to die after bestowing his immortal powers on Promethius.

Although Chiron was unable to heal his own wounds, he became a wise healer, physician, teacher and musician. He was mentor to Jason, Achilles, Hercules and other Greek heros. Chiron is also credited for discovering homoeopathy and the medicinal use of plants.

Chiron was an intelligent, civilized and kind centaur; so he was unlike other centaurs, which perhaps accentuated his sense of being an outsider. Perhaps Chiron, like the Punk Monk, is "the outsiders' outsider", and not altogether accepted by his brethren.

The journey of *The Wounded Healer*, therefore, is about living with a painful wound, and developing wisdom and healing powers to benefit others. Consistent with the principle of homoeopathy - the poison is the antidote – so the wound is used positively and selflessly to help others.

In 1977 a new planet was discovered by astronomer Charles T. Kowal of the Hale Laboratories in California. The planet became known as Chiron, The Wounded Healer, due to its energetic resonance with the mythological centaur and the consciousness of Christ.

The planet Chiron was discovered in the year that punk rock exploded in UK. Between 1976 and 1978 several underground protests rose to the surface of public consciousness, including gay rights in America and the formation of Adult Children of Alcoholics (ACoA).

Dionysus, The Greek Party God

Centaurs follow Dionysus, the Greek God of nature, fertility, wine and spiritual intoxication. Dionysus is the party God, lover of wine, women and song, and sex and drugs and rock and roll.

Punks and shamans dance to tribal rhythms. Shamans ingest hallucinogens while they dance in a state of trance. Punks often use the pogo dance in a cathartic state.

Dionysus, also known as Bacchus and *"The Liberator"*, is the God of *"foreign origins"*. So Dionysus is also the God of exiles, outsiders and aliens. The Liberator, son of Zeus, uses music to transform stress and worry into pure uplifting energy; and punk music serves this purpose effectively.

Hades

Hades is the Greek God of the underworld, a place familiar to most punks and shamans. Black sheep were ritually sacrificed in honor of Hades.

216

Hephaestus, The Ugly God of Fire

Hephaestus is the Greek God of fire[6], volcanoes and blacksmiths' furnaces, and patron of craftsmen. Hephaestus' burning fire[12] is said to be represented externally by the blacksmiths' furnace.[1]

Hephaestus was born ugly[2], weak and crippled. Myth states that the God of fire was conceived parthenogenetically[7] by Hera, without fertilization by her partner, Zeus. Hera's conception of Hephaestus was an act of vengeance towards Zeus for fathering Athena with Metis.

Hera was so disgusted by the sight of her deformed baby that she threw him from Mount Olympus[5]. Hephaestus' fall down the mountain lasted a whole day before he landed in the sea where he was nursed to recovery by water nymphs. The fall caused Hephaestus to have a lame leg.

So, like the centaur, Chiron, Hephaestus was wounded and rejected by his mother. Other accounts state that it was Zeus who threw Hephaestus from Mount Olympus; and he landed on the island of Lemnos where he resided in a palace with his foundries at the foot of the volcano, Mount Etna.

Hephaestus took revenge on his mother for abandoning him; he forged a magic throne to entrap her. The throne was presented to Hera on Mount Olympus, and when she sat on it she was ensnared.[4] Hephaestus refused to release his mother despite pleas from fellow gods. Eventually Hera was released after winning Aphrodite[9] as his bride.

The fire god was renowned as a fine craftsman and blacksmith.[3] Hephaestus manufactured thunderbolts for Zeus, invincible armor for Achilles and forged the chains which bound Prometheus to a rock. The blacksmith even forged golden handmaidens[8] who subsequently assisted him in his workshop.

Hephaestus formed Pandora, the first mortal woman, by molding earth and water together. Pandora is popularly known for opening a jar against strict instructions not to do so. Pandora was compelled by her natural curiosity to discover the contents of the jar. Instantly, evil spirits escaped from the container, darkening the entire planet. Although the demonic forces had fled, there remained hope at the base of the vessel.

Hephaestus is the god of creative self-expression[10] and individuality. Like Chiron, Hephaestus was both wounded and abandoned; but Hephaestus helps others to express their creativity using metal and other materials. However, the fire god's physical impediments and family rebuttal did not crush his will to succeed in his endeavors.[11]

Aphrodite, Hephaestus' wife, committed adultery on several occasions. So Hephaestus engineered an infallible and invisible chain-linked net to entrap[4] Aphrodite with her adulterous partners. When Aphrodite slept with Ares, the god of war, Hephaestus threw the magic net over the couple and hauled them to the Olympian gods.

The god of fire is depicted as an ugly cripple bent over his blacksmith's anvil. Homer describes Hephaestus as walking with the aid of a stick. However Hephaestus was a peaceful and kind god who contributed greatly to craftsmanship and metallurgy.

Hermes, The Trickster God of Thieves

Hermes is the Greek trickster God of thievery, communication and duplicity. The son of Zeus and Goddess Maia from Pleiades, Hermes was born a mortal though he desperately desired immortality.[14]

On the day of Hades' birth he discovered a tortoise with spangled shell outside his cave. The infant immediately lopped off the creatures' limbs and created a lyre – an ancient Greek harp – from its shell. Within hours the baby was strumming the instrument with artistic prowess.

During the same day, Hermes left his crib to find meat to quell his hunger. The infant stole Apollo's cattle, sacrificed them and cooked twelve portions of meat. Apollo asked Hermes to confess his thievery while he was cradled amongst blankets. When Apollo called Hermes *"The Prince of Thieves"*, Hermes farted and sneezed, but still refused to admit his crime.

Eventually Apollo and Zeus found evidence of Hermes' dishonesty, so the infant had to confess to his misdemeanors. Hades defended himself by telling Zeus that he had sacrificed the cattle in honor of the twelve Gods; requesting that he become the twelfth God. Zeus agreed to bestow divinity upon Hermes.

Later Hermes gave his lyre to Apollo as a form of settlement; and he even taught Apollo how to play the instrument. Apollo and Hermes became good friends, and Apollo gave Hermes his golden caduceus, the symbol for wellbeing.

The trickster God promised Zeus that he would not lie again, even though he could not vow to tell the entire truth. Zeus proclaimed Hermes to be the God of communication, commerce, advertising, public relations and all other forms of duplicity.

John Peel

John Peel is the British God of the airwaves, mediation and indie rock.

"I never make stupid mistakes - only very, very clever ones"
- John Peel

John Peel, born in 1939 as John Robert Parker Ravenscroft, is the legendary folk hero from Merseyside, down-to-earth BBC Radio disc jockey for upcoming grassroots indie rock music, and unorthodox broadcaster with a massive cult following. John died of heart attack in Peru at the age of 65 in 2004.

John Peel is John's nom de plume for his public broadcasting career. The three-syllable surname, Ravenscroft, was considered too long and aristocratic for his audience.

John is known for his ironic humor, adolescent pranks and his passion for seminal music. However, despite his middle class upbringing, he was humble, often self-deprecating and sensitive. John Peel stands out from his egocentric peers due to his laid-back eccentric style and his integrity.

"I've always found it easier to tell the truth because that way you don't have to remember what you said. So, for purely practical reasons, it's the best thing."
- John Peel.

220

John Peel had a lonely and emotionally-deprived childhood. He was sent away to boarding school in Shrewsbury where he was raped and bullied. The lack of love in his upbringing was reflected in his self-effacing demeanor and lack of confidence.

His school housemaster described John as exceptionally eccentric. In his autobiography called *Margrave of the Marshes*, John Peel's wife, Sheila, described one of his idiosyncrasies as saving his toenail clippings (because he believed that one day they might be valuable).

John developed his Liverpudlian accent, partially as a knee-jerk reaction against his cold middle class roots, but also as a bridge to supporters of The Beatles who came from Liverpool. John's local accent enhanced his appeal amongst his fans.[16]

John and his wife Sheila (nicknamed Pig) established a tightly-knit and happy family at their home known as *"Peel Acres"* in Suffolk.

John Peel was a passionate *"divining rod"* of talented alternative rock bands. His favorite post punk band was The Fall. Mark E. Smith is the erratic front-man and founder of The Fall.

John Peel created havoc at the radio station when he publicly admitted to having a sexually transmitted disease. However, he was so popular that the management of BBC Radio was unable to fire him. Later he presented a family phone-in program called *Home Truths* on BBC Radio 4. One of the laudable goals of Home Truths was to resolve differences between family members.

221

John Peel's awards include: *The Godlike Genius Award* (New Musical Express, 1994); voted disc jockey of the year eleven times by Melody Maker magazine; he was voted 43rd *"Greatest Briton Of All Times"* in a poll by BBC; and an OBE for his services to British music, 1998.

Above all, John Peel was a real individual who never sold out. True to John's request, the song *"Teenage Kicks"* by The Undertones was played loudly at his funeral. And on his tombstone, underneath his name, are the lyrics *"TEENAGE DREAMS, SO HARD TO BEAT!"*

Kali

Kali is the Hindu goddess of destruction known as *"The Black One."*

Kali, a symbol for the destructive aspect of the goddess Mahadevi, has a gruesome appearance: an emaciated figure with a long blood-craving tongue and wearing a necklace of skulls.

Kali is commonly depicted as dancing around the sexually aroused corpse of her husband Shiva. She symbolizes the will to destroy and her devotees ritually sacrifice humans.

The Black One was created to kill demons who threaten the cosmic order. Many negative aspects of humanity need Kali's intent to destroy, such as ignorance, illusion, greed and arrogance.

Perhaps the energy of Kali cajoled The Sex Pistols to lambast the British monarchy in their anarchic song, *"God save the Queen"*, and Princess Diana to burst the Royals' romantic bubble of illusion. Johnny Rotten unleashed intense ferocity upon the Royal family in this masterpiece.

Loki

Loki is the Norse God of trickery and mischief.

Sisyphus

Sisyphus, proletarian of the gods, powerless and rebellious, knows the whole extent of his wretched condition; it is what he thinks of during his wretched descent. The lucidity that was to constitute his torture at the same time crowns his victory. There is no fate that cannot be surmounted by scorn.
- Albert Camus

THE PUNK MONK QUOTIENT

Take the following multiple-choice test to find out your
Punk Monk Quotient:

1. Specialization

A   I am an expert in my field
B   I am a "Jack of all Trades"
C   I want to be a specialist

2. Competition

A   I am competitive
B   I buy out my competition
C   I am not very competitive

3. Relationships

A   I have many friends
B   I have an elitist social network
C   I choose fewer deeper relationships

4. Credit

A   I borrow as much as possible
B   I try to avoid credit
C   I try to enhance my credit status

5. Behavior

A   I adapt my behavior to fit each situation
B   I do not change my behavior for anyone
C   I respect bigots

6. Ambition

A I want to be rich
B I want to achieve my full potential
C I want to be famous

7. Gossip Columns

A I read gossip columns about celebrities
B I am not interested in celebrity gossip
C I like to follow fashion and trends

8. The News

A I believe the news I read in newspapers
B I don't believe everything I read in newspapers
C All media coverage is false

9. Motivation

A I am motivated by money and status
B I am self-directed by my Soul
C I am motivated by peer pressure

10. Religion

A I am religious
B I believe in God or a Higher Power
C I am not sure about God or religion

11. Time & Money

A I have more money than time
B I have more time than money
C Time is money

12. Independence

A   I value being part of an organization
B   I value my independence
C   I value rigid structure

13. Respect

A   I respect people who are successful
B   I respect people who have integrity
C   I respect everyone equally

14. Freedom

A   Freedom is being successful
B   Freedom is being authentic
C   Freedom is being financially secure

15. Intimacy

A   I relate with people to fulfill my needs
B   I am attracted by a person's essence
C   I am attracted by a person's status

16. Science & Art

A   If science cannot explain it, forget it
B   There is much that science cannot explain
C   Artists are inferior to scientists

17. Progress

A   Real progress is an enhanced economy
B   Real progress is happiness and enlightenment
C   Globalization enables real progress

18. Structure

A   I trust authorities and respect rules and laws
B   Authorities are prone to corruption
C   I believe in hierarchy

19. Life Purpose

A   My goal is to be rich and famous
B   My goal is to express myself creatively
C   My goal is to be immortal

20. Personality

A   I am smart, cool and connected
B   I am an individual, and perhaps eccentric
C   I always tow the line

21. Family

A   I have the full support of my family
B   I am the black sheep of my family
C   Everyone should honor their parents

22. Originality

A   It doesn't matter how you achieve the goal
B   I do it my way or not at all
C   I don't have enough money to be authentic

23. Unity

A   I believe in a prosperous world
B   I believe in a unified world
C   Unity is impossible

24. Standardization

A   Standardization is efficient
B   Every person is unique
C   I live by formulae

25. Communication

A   I am politically correct
B   I speak the truth, even if it hurts
C   I need to tell lies to survive

26. Psychic Ability

A   I am completely normal
B   I am psychic
C   I have learning difficulties

27. Growth

A   I believe in leveraged growth using credit
B   I believe in organic growth
C   I do not believe in growth

28. Energy

A   I believe in renewable energy (eg wind farms)
B   I believe in fossil fuel (oil and petrol)
C   I believe in nuclear power

29. Drugs

A   Drugs can facilitate personal growth
B   Drugs are for losers
C   Use of drugs is immoral

30. Revenge

A   Revenge is sweet
B   I harm myself when I take revenge
C   Revenge is justice

31. Immortality

A   I do not mind when I die
B   I want to live forever
C   I feel immortal

32. Retirement

A   I work(ed) to live
B   I live(d) to work
C   I work(ed) for my retirement

33. Love

A   I believe in true love
B   True love is an illusion
C   True love is negotiated

34. Empowerment

A   I am self-empowered
B   I am a victim
C   Our fate is determined at birth

35 Winning

A   Winning is more important than truth
B   It doesn't matter how you win
C   Truth is more important than winning

DETERMINING YOUR PUNK MONK QUOTIENT (SCORE)

Use the table below to calculate your Punk Monk Quotient.

QUESTION #	A	B	C
1	-1	+1	-1
2	0	-1	+1
3	0	-1	+1
4	-1	+1	-1
5	0	+1	-1
6	0	+1	-1
7	0	+1	-1
8	-1	0	+1
9	0	+1	-1
10	-1	+1	0
11	-1	+1	0
12	0	+1	-1
13	0	+1	0
14	-1	+1	0
15	0	+1	-1
16	-1	+1	-1
17	0	+1	-1
18	-1	0	-1
19	-1	+1	0
20	0	+1	-1
21	0	+1	-1
22	-1	+1	-1
23	0	+1	-1

24	0	+1	-1
25	-1	+1	0
26	0	+1	0
27	-1	+1	0
28	+1	0	-1
29	+1	0	-1
30	-1	+1	0
31	+1	-1	0
32	+1	-1	0
33	+1	-1	-1
34	+1	-1	0
35	-1	-1	+1

Naturally a high score is indicative of Punk Monk characteristics, non-conformity and 'outsider-dom'; and a low (or negative score) is scored by insiders and people holding traditional beliefs.

If your score is over +20 you are a Punk Monk, but if your score is under -15 you are highly resistant to change.

DISCOGRAPHY: GREAT PUNK / NEW WAVE
TUNES Selected by Phil Nicks

NAME OF SONG	NAME OF BAND
1977	The Clash
Anarchy In The UK	The Sex Pistols
Barbarism Begins at Home	The Smiths
Billericay Dickie	Ian Drury & the Blockheads
Blue Monday	New Order
California Uber Alles	The Dead Kennedys
China Girl	Iggy Pop / David Bowie
Dance this Mess Around	The B52s
E = MC2	Big Audio Dynamite
Friction	Television
Genius of Love	Tom Tom Club
God Save The Queen	The Sex Pistols
Holiday in Cambodia	The Dead Kennedys
Kung Fu International	John Cooper-Clarke
London Calling	The Clash
Make Believe Mambo	David Byrne
Mesopotamia	The B52s
Miami Nice	Elastica
Oh Bondage, Up Yours!	X-Ray Spex
Once In A Lifetime	Talking Heads
Party out of Bounds	The B52s
Passable / A Past Gone Mad	The Fall
Passenger, The	Iggy Pop
PDA	Interpol
Police and Thieves	The Clash
Problems	The Sex Pistols

NAME OF SONG	NAME OF BAND
Reward	Teardrop Explodes
Roxette	Dr Feelgood
Smash it Up!	The Damned
Smile Like You Mean It	The Killers
Tattooed Love Boys	The Pretenders
Terry Waite Sez	The Fall
That's Entertainment	The Jam
The Charming Man	The Smiths
Transmission	Joy Division
Typical Girls	The Slits
Wot	Captain Sensible

NOTES & REFERENCES

CHAPTER 1

1. Answers.com, 18 July 2009
2. Dictionary.com, 18 July 18, 2009
3. Allwords.com, 18 July 2009
4. Knowledgerush.com, 18 July 2009
5. Thefreedictionary.com, 18 July 2009
6. Merriam-webster.com, 18 July 2009
7. Thesaurus, 18 July 2009
8. Yourdictionary.com, 18 July 2009
9. Audioenglish.net, 18 July
10. Synonym.com, 18 July 18, 2009
11. See (10)
12. Onlineslangdictionary.com, 18 July 18, 2009
13. See (12)
14. Idoceonline.com, 18 July 18, 2009
15. Answers.yahoo.com, 18 July 18, 2009
16. Wikipedia.com, 18 July 2009
17. Reverso dictionary, 18 July 2009
18. Allwords.com, 18 July 18, 2009
19. Urbandictionary.com, 18 July 18, 2009
20. See (7) above
21. Answerbag.com, 18 July 2009
22. Wordreference.com, 18 July 2009
23. See (7) cf.
24. See (6) cf.
25. See (2) cf.
26. See (2) cf.
27. Questia.com, 19 July 2009
28. Springhousecandles.com, 19 July 2009
29. Barkeaters.com, 19 July 2009
30. Amazon.com/spunk-official

31. Answers.com, 19 July 2009

32. Designboom.com/eng/interview/byrne.html

33. Musicstack.com, 19 July 2009

34. *The Future is Unwritten*, a documentary about Joe Strummer

35. Yahoo.answers.com, 19 July 2009

36. *"Such, Such were the days"*, George Orwell

37. Jim derogates, www.jimdero.com/otherwritings/other-strokes, 31 July 2009

38. Maureen Cleave, interview with John Lennon, Evening Standard, 4 March 1966 (p378, *The Mammoth Book of Journalism*, Edited by Jon E. Lewis, Carroll & Graf)

39. Nietzche, *Thus Spoke Zarathustra*

40. Songfacts.com, 30 July 2009

41. www.wisdomquotes.com

42. *Tattooed Love Boys* was published on The Pretenders (debut album) in 1980

43. P148, Gilbert, Pat, *Passion is a Fashion ~ The real story of The Clash*, Aurum Press Ltd

44. from the song, *"Problems"* by The Sex Pistols, from the album, *Never Mind The Bollocks* (1977)

45. P5-8, Gilbert, Pat, *Passion is a Fashion ~ The real story of The Clash*, Aurum Press Ltd

46. from the album, *"Germ-free Adolescents"*, x-rayspex.com (the official website of X-ray Spex)

47. Two or five chocolate fingers are standard on Nestle's *Kit-Kat* bar

48. *"Rebel Without A Cause"* is a song by Tom Petty and the Heartbreakers

49. *"Smash It Up!"* is a song by The Damned

50. Article by Sean O'Hagan, The Observer 3 March 2002

51. Lyrics from the song, *"Party Out Of Bounds"* from the B52s' album, *"Wild Planet"* (1980)

235

52. from the song, *"Lost in Music"* from the album *"The Infotainment Scan*
53. Tony Fletcher's Jamming magazines is available on-line at www.ijamming.net
54. Jacobi
55. Quote by Johnny Rotten (John Lydon) of The Sex Pistols
56. *"24 Hour Party People"* is a film about Manchester's punk rock scene, directed by Michael Winterbottom and released 2002.
57. http://www.superseventies.com/ac27aladdinsane.htm 6 July 2009
58. Interview with Poly Styrene by Charlotte Philby, The Independent, Saturday, 19 April 2008
59. The UK band, Crass, launched a massive demonstration against Margaret Thatcher's invasion of the Falkland Islands in 1982.
60. Francis, Eric, http://planetwaves.net/smallworlds/contents/planets/chiron.html, 10 October 2009
61. The Stranglers, *"Ugly"*
62. *La Poloma* – Longing Worldwide, musical documentary, directed by Sigrid Faltin (2008)
63. Babynamespedia.com, 16 Nov 2009
64. musicroom.com, 16 Nov 2009
65. Picture Dick Interview, 1984
66. Bangs, Lester, "The Clash", *Let Fury have the Hour ~ The Punk Rock Politics of Joe Strummer*, Nation Books (2004) p71
67. Salewicz, Chris, *Redemption Song ~ The Definitive Biography of Joe Strummer,* Harper (2007), p199
68. Salewicz, Chris, *Redemption Song ~ The Definitive Biography of Joe Strummer,* Harper (2007), p199
69. Salewicz, Chris, *Redemption Song ~ The Definitive Biography of Joe Strummer*, Harper (2007), p198

70. http://www.crispinsartwell.com/punkphilosophy.htm
71. http://en.wikipedia.org/wiki/Florence_Foster_Jenkins
72. The Guardian, 15 January 2005

CHAPTER 2

1. P3, Feuerstein, Georg PhD., *Holy Madness*, Penguin Arkana
2. p52-53, Hyde, Lewis, T*rickster makes the World ~ Mischief, Myth and Art,* FSG New York
3. p54, Hyde, Lewis, *Trickster makes the World ~ Mischief, Myth and Art*, FSG New York
4. p23, Kohn, Alfie, *Unconditional Parenting ~ Moving from Rewards and Punishment to Love and Reason*, Atria Books
5. The song *"Framed"* is on the live album, *The Sensational Alex Harvey Band Live.*
6. Chinen, Allan, www.angelfire.com, 19 October 2009
7. "Passable" from the album, "27 Points" by The Fall
8. p110, The Yoruba system is similar to the I Ching, Hyde, Lewis, *Trickster makes the World ~ Mischief, Myth and Art*, FSG New York
9. Page 92, *Passion is a Fashion ~ The real story of The Clash*, by Pat Gilbert
10. p38, Ballinger, Franchot, *Living Sideways*
11. The Future is Unwritten (a documentary about Joe Strummer) directed by Julian Temple
12. p39, Ballinger, Franchot, *Living Sideways*
13. Issan is a province in the northeast of Thailand where the US Army based its R & R services during the Vietnam war
14. Courtney Love is the female punk rocker from the band Hole, and girlfriend of the legendary Kurt Cobain (singer and songwriter of grunge band Nirvana) who died of a drug overdose in 1994

15. *Love Precepts* by Phil Nicks (www.philnicks.com), published by Citylife magazine

16. Nicks, Phil, *Love Entrepreneurs ~ Cross-Culture Relationship Deals in Thailand*, fasttrackpublishing.com

17. Rutzky, Jacques, *The Trickster Archetype in Psychotherapy with Alcoholics and Addicts* (www.cgjung-page.com) (Sandner, 1979, Henderson, 1959)

18. *"That's Entertainment"* is a song by punk band, The Jam, about urban violence

19. Excerpt from the film, *24 Hour Party People*, directed by Michael Winterbottom, 2001

20. p36, Hyde, Lewis, *Trickster makes the World ~ Mischief, Myth and Art*, FSG New York

21. p44, Hathaway, Nancy, *The Friendly Guide to Mythology*, Penguin Books

22. p47, Hathaway, Nancy, *The Friendly Guide to Mythology*, Penguin Books

23. Lydon, John, *No Irish, No Blacks, No Dogs* (biography of Johnny Rotten)

24. Simpson, Dave, *The Fallen*, www.thefallenbook.co.uk

25. Scientology was pioneered by Ron Hubbard, author of Dianetics

26. p68, Feuerstein, Georg PhD., *Holy Madness*, Penguin Arkana

27. Osho's "social meditations" include *The Dynamic* and *Kundalini*

28. p39, Osho, Tantra: *The Supreme Understanding*

29. p19-20, Hyde, Lewis, *Trickster makes the World ~ Mischief, Myth and Art*, FSG New York

30. p40, Hassan, Steven, *Combatting Cult Mind Control*, Park Street Press

31. p209, Bierhorst, John, *The Mythology of South America*, Quill William Morrow

32. p111, Osho, *Meetings with Remarkable People*, Wat-

kins Publishing
33. p122-123, Bierhorst, John, T*he Mythology of South America*, Quill William Morrow
34. p125, as above (33)
35. Adolf Hitler had a similar vision, inspired by Frederick Nietzsche's *"Will as Power"* philosophy to support his pursuit of Aryan supremacy and the extermination of six million Jews
36. Mark, Chapter 11: verses 15 – 17; Matthew, Chapter 21; and Luke, Chapter 19
37. New Testament, Mark, Chapter 4, verse 5; Matthew, Chapter 13, Verse 5
38. *"The Monk and The Drunk"*, *Sweet and Sour Tales from China*, retold by Carol Kendall and Yao-wen Li, Houghton Mifflin/Clarion/New York, re-retold by Phil Nicks
39. Sartwell, Crispin, crispinsartwell.com/punkphilosophy.com, 24 Nov 2009
40. Alternativetentacles.com, 24 Nov 2009
41. "Porky pie" is a term meaning untruth
42. Lyrics from the song, *The Magnificent Seven*, from the album, *Sandinista* by The Clash
43. Blake, William, *The Marriage of Heaven and Hell*
44. mythweb.com, 28 Nov 2009
45. Byrne, David, *Good and Evil* is from the album, *Rei Momo* from which proceeds were tithed for the regeneration of the Amazonian rain forest

CHAPTER 3

1. http://www.merriam-webster.com/dictionary/outsiders Date: 3 Nov 2009
2. http://thesaurus.reference.com/browse/outsider, 3 Nov 2009
3. Orwell, George, *Nineteen Eighty Four*

4. Marr, Johnny, guitarist of The Smiths, The Outsiders: *Johnny Marr on the misfits and mavericks who make music magical*, The Independent, 14 November 2008 ~ an edited version of Johnny Marr's lecture at the University of Salford, entitled, Always from the Outside: Mavericks, Innovators and Building your Own Ark.
5. Wikipedia, 3 November 2009
6. Cope, Julian, *Black Sheep Album*, released 8 September 2009
7. See (6) above
8. Chaline, Eric, *The Book of Gods & Goddesses*, Harper Collins (2004)
9. Wilson, Colin, *The Outsider*, Picador, p25
10. *'Confusion'* is from New Order's album, *Substance* (1987)
11. *Boys don't Cry* is an album by The Cure
12. Wilson, Colin, *The Outsider*, Picador, p159
13. Algren, Nelson, *A Walk on the Wild Side*, 1956
14. Kohn, Alfie, *Unconditional Parenting ~ Moving from Rewards and Punishments to Love and Reason*, Atria Books, p23
15. Encyclopedia.com, 14 November 2009
16. The Stranglers, *Peaches* from the album, *Rattus Norwegicus*
17. www.news.scotsman.com, 7 November 2009
18. Gilbert, Pat, *Passion is a Fashion ~ The Real Story of The Clash*, Aurum (2005)
19. Simpson, Mark, *Saint Morrissey*, Touchstone, New York (2006)
20. Brainyquote.com, 8 November 2009
21. *Soul Mining* is an album title by The The, fronted by outsider artist Matt Johnson
22. The Fall, from the song, *Paranoia Man in Cheap Shit Room*
23. Tony Wilson was acted by Steve Coogan in Manches-

ter's punk documentary *24 Hour Party People*, directed by Julien Temple

24. Lyrics from *Free Range,* from The Falls' *Code Selfish* album with reference to Frederick Nietzsche's book, *Thus Spoke Zarathustra*, which was misinterpreted by the Nazis in their pursuit of Aryan supremacy

25. Lightbody Integration is a healing modality practiced by Nicolas Guy Ngan who specializes in walk-ins

26. Larkin, Emma, *Finding George Orwell in Burma*, Penguin (2004), p69

27. Beadon, see (26) above.

28. The Smiths, *Meat is Murder* album

29. Forward, Dr Susan, *Toxic Parents ~ Overcoming their Hurtful Legacy and reclaiming your Life*, Bantam Books (1990), P6

30. Robert Smith, songwriter and vocalist of The Cure, was given the New Musical Express 'Godlike Genius' award in 2002 (TBC)

31. Simpson, Mark, *Saint Morrissey*, Touchstone, New York (2006), p245

32. Bowker, George, *Inside George Orwell*,

33. Larkin, Emma, *Finding George Orwell in Burma*, Penguin (2004), p93

34. O'Connor, Michael, http://contemporarylit.about.com, review for about.com

35. D'Ambtosio, Antonino, *Let Fury have the Hour ~ the Punk Politics of Joe Strummer*, Nation Books, p29

36. Hopkins, Jerry, The Lizard King (1992)

37. The author visited Rio de Janeiro in the eighties and met an acquaintance of Biggs who socialized with him regularly on Rio's party circuit

38. Lyrics from *Give my Compliments to the Chef* from The Sensational Alex Harvey Band (SAHB) Live album

39. Lyrics by The Smiths from *Nowhere Fast*,

40. D'Ambtosio, Antonino, *Let Fury have the Hour ~ the Punk Politics of Joe Strummer*, Nation Books (2004), Pxxi

41. Gilbert, Pat, *Passion is a Fashion ~ The Real Story of The Clash*, Aurum (2005) p8

42. *The Future is Unwritten*, a documentary about Joe Strummer, directed by Julien Temple

43. Lyrics from the song, *Parents* by Budgie

44. Owen, Glen, The Day John Peel was Raped, Mail on Sunday (www.dailymail.co.uk) and *Margrave of the Marshes* by John Peel and Shiela Ravenscroft (the official autobiography of John Peel)

45. Waters, Roger, *Another Brick in the Wall, Part 2*, from the album The Wall (1979)

46. Blue Oyster Cult, lyrics from the song, *This ain't the Summer of Love*, from the album, *Agents of Fortune*

47. *The Future is Unwritten*, a documentary about Joe Strummer, directed by Julien Temple

48. Blake, William, *The Marriage of Heaven and Hell*

49. The movie *Birdy*, which was directed by Alan Parker, is based on the novel *Birdy* by William Wharton. The movie was released in 1985.

CHAPTER 4

Hawkins, David R., M.D., PhD., (2005) *Power Vs Force ~ The Hidden Determinants of Human Behavior*, Hay House

Holden, Dr Robert, *Happiness Now!*, Hay House

Layard, R (2005), *Happiness: Lessons from a New Science*, Penguin Press

New Economics Foundation, Neweconomics.org

Prawase, W (2004), *Redefining Progress*, Outlook, The Bangkok Post

CHAPTER 5

Monkey Business in Southeast Asia is based upon selected case studies from Chapter 10 of *How to Establish a Successful Business in Thailand* by Philip Wylie, published by Paiboon Publishing (Paiboonpublishing.com)

CHAPTER 6

The Land of Philip was written by Phil Nicks on a journalistic tirade in Manila and Baguio between 25 July 2006 and 15 August 2006. Reference was made to Rev. Alex Orbito's book, *Born to Heal.*

The Ghost's Vanishing Cap was originally told by Maung Htin Aung

CHAPTER 7

The Kammu Orphan was originally translated and retold by Kristina Lindell who was a researcher with the Scandinavian Institute of Asian Studies.

Tricksters of the Night contains excerpts from Phil Nicks's *Love Entrepreneurs* (ISBN 978-616-90336-0-8) published by Fast Track Publishing. The chapter, *Gender Illusionists*, is based upon an interview with author Jerry Hopkins by Phil Nicks.

GLOSSARY

1. Ron Leadbetter, Pantheon.org/articles/h/Hephaestus. html
2. Joe Strummer, vocalist of punk band, The Clash, commented about punk, "…if you're ugly, you're in!"
3. There is a connection between Hephaestus' work as a blacksmith and the The Punk Monk's alchemical transformation of base materials into gold.
4. Refer to the Trickster archetype
5. Abandonment and social exclusion are core themes in the punk movement and the Punk Monk; many monks and novices in Thailand are orphans
6. The Roman god of fire - which is based upon the Greek myth of Hephaestus – is known as Vulcan
7. The Punk Monk was also conceived without fertilization by his mother's husband; instead, his mother was sired by an alien from the planet Chiron
8. Hamilton, Edith, Mythology ~ Timeless Tales of Gods and Heroes, Mentor Books, p 35
9. Hephaestus' wife was called Aphrodite in the Odyssey; and Aglaia in Hesiod in The Iliad (reference as in (8) above)
10. Creative self-expression and individually is the basis of punk culture
11. Reinhart, Melanie, Chiron and Wounded Healer, p111
12. The burning fire represents innate angst which is typically transformed by punks into creative self-expression
13. Hathaway, Nancy, The Friendly Guide to Mythology, p232,
14. See (13) above, p233-235
15. See (13) above, p193-194
16. PhD thesis about the effect of accent upon broadcasting audience, University of Liverpool

OTHER BIBLIOGRAPHICAL REFERENCES

Armstrong, Thomas, *The Natural Genius of Children*, http://www.thomasarmstrong.com/natural_genius.htm

Bair, Deirdre, *Jung: A Biography*, Back Bay Books

Ballinger, Franchot, *Living Sideways*

Blake, William, *The Echoing Green*

Blake, William, *The Marriage of Heaven and Hell*

Boeree, Dr C. George, Carl Jung, http://webspace.ship. edu/cgboer/jung.html 8 June 2009

Charan Singh, Shiv (2004), *Let the Numbers Guide You – The spiritual Science of Numerology*, O-Books

Forward, Dr Susan, *Toxic Parents ~ Overcoming their hurtful legacy and reclaiming your life*, Bantam Books

Geldof, Sir Bob, *Is that it?*

Hamilton, Edith, *Mythology ~ Timeless Tales of Gods and Heroes*, Mentor Books

Hicks, Esther & Jerry, *Laws of Attraction ~ Basics of the Teachings of Abraham*, Hay House Inc

Initiates of Hermes, *The Kybalion*, The Yogi Publication Society

Johncooperclarke.com, *Kung Fu International* (20 May 2009)

John-Roger, *Psychic Protection*, Mandeville Press

Jung C. G., *Memories, Dreams, Reflections*, Fontana Press

Kenya-advisor.com, *The Masai Jumping Dance*

O'Hara, Craig, *The Philosophy of Punk: More than Noise*, AK Press

Orwell, George, *Such, Such were the Joys*

Pavlov, I. P. (1927). *Conditioned Reflexes: An Investigation of the Physiological Activity of the Cerebral Cortex.* Translated and Edited by G. V. Anrep. London: Oxford University Press.

Peel, John: *Margrave of The Marshes*, John Peel & Shiela Ravenscroft

Plotkin, Bill, *Soulcraft ~ Crossing into the Mysteries of Nature and Psyche*, New World Library

http://planetwaves.net/astrology/virgoastrology.html

Reinhart, Melanie, *Chiron and the Healing Journey, An Astrological and Psychological Perspective*, Penguin Arkana

Roberts, Maureen B PhD, *Re-visioning Soul Retrieval: The Spectrum of active and Passive Healing in Shamanism and Jungian Psychotherapy*, Jungcircle.com

Rossiter, Altazar PhD (2006), *Developing Spiritual intelligence ~ The Power of You*, O-Books

Sartwell, Crispin, *Philosophy of Punk*, crispinsartwell. com/ punkphilosophy.htm|

Sharamon, S & Baginski J, *The Chakra Handbook*, Motilal Banarsidass Publishers

Tolle, Eckhart, *A New Earth ~ Awakening to your Life's Purpose*, Penguin Group (Plume, USA)

Vatican: *It's OK to believe in Aliens*, The Associated Press

OTHER BOOKS FROM FAST TRACK PUBLISHING

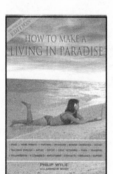

Fax (Hong Kong): +852-3010-9769
Email: fasttrackpublishing@gmail.com